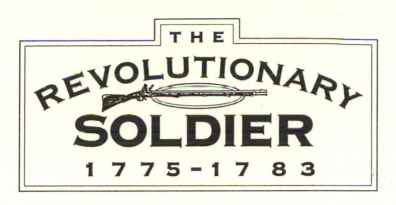

C. Keith Wilbur's Illustrated Living History Series

THE ILLUSTRATED LIVING HISTORY SERIES

THE REVOLUTIONARY SOLDIER 1775-1783

An Illustrated Sourcebook of Authentic Details about
Everyday Life for Revolutionary War Soldiers

C. Keith Wilbur

The Globe Pequot Press

Guilford, Connecticut

Library of Congress Cataloging-in-Publication Data
Wilbur, C. Keith, 1923-
  The revolutionary soldier, 1775-1783 : an illustrated sourcebook
of authentic details about everyday life for Revolutionary War
soldiers / by C. Keith Wilbur. — 1st Globe Pequot ed.
    p. cm.—(The illustrated living history series)
Includes bibliographical references and index.
ISBN 978-1-56440-166-3
1. United States. Continental Army—Military life. 2. Soldiers—
United States—History—18th century. 3. United States—Militia—
History—18th century. 4. United States—HIstory—Revolution,
1775-1783—Antiquities. 1. Title. II. Series.
E259.W52 1993
973.3'8—dc20   92-40011
                                                              CIP

REVOLUTIONARY SOLDER

Manufactured in the United States of America
First Lyons Press edition/Eleventh Printing

Contents

PREFACE

Silver eagle worn on Washington's hat cockade.

A mother and her two sons stood before a museum display case that contained relics of the Revolutionary War. "And there", she said, pointing matter-of-factly toward a wrought iron bullet mold, "is a thing the soldiers used to crack nuts."

This volume was conceived as soon as the horror of the moment had passed. In it one may find drawings that an itinerant quill and ink sketcher might make on a visit to the Continental Army camp~including bullet molds! Generally, these represent a composite of the uniform and equipment and the heroic men who used them. In a few instances, specific and unusual articles and their sources are noted.

Thank heaven for those who had the foresight to preserve our past in the nation's museums! The relics are there for you and I to see, and with a wider eye to visualize the courageous soldiers who carried them and fought for freedom in those trying times.

MILITIAMEN

All able-bodied men between 16 and 60 were members of the state militia. Filling short-term enlistments, they appeared on the camp scene at irregular intervals. They brought with them a confusing array of drill commands from the home town musters, frequently spiced with the militiaman's own improvements on loading and firing.

These rugged individualists were at their best when skirmishing on their own initiative in the American forests. But a standardized drill and discipline were necessary before they could join the Continental soldier in stalling a determined British charge.

Each state required its militiamen to furnish themselves with such equipment as a flintlock and bayonet or sword or tomahawk, priming brush and pick, pouch or cartridge box, gun flints, knapsack, blanket, canteen or wooden bottle - and often a jack knife.

GROWING PAINS IN THE ARMY

Far more was needed than the temporary help from the militia if liberty was to become a reality. In 1776, Congress, prodded by Washington, resolved to raise a standing army with enlistments for three years or the duration of the war. Each state had its quota of soldiers to fill, and inducements included a bounty, wages, uniforms, and one hundred acres of land. A private's pay for one month was $6.67.

But Congress was without power to enforce such requests from the states. Enlistments lagged and clothing and weapons were in scanty supply. The few uniforms available rapidly turned to tatters without replacements. As an officer in Stark's Brigade put it, there was "many a good lad with nothing to cover him from his hips to his toes save his blanket."

To make matters worse, those patriotic Americans who joined the Continental ranks found their Continental pay had depreciated from thirty dollars paper money to one dollar of hard coin. In like straits, the army could not afford proper food, and hunger seemed to be part of the daily camp routine.

CLOTHING THE TROOPS

The knotty problem of clothing the troops was partly solved by Washington's observations of his riflemen. Through his urging, Congress recommended that rifle shirts be included in the clothing bounty.

As early as his General Order of July 24, 1776, he pointed out the practicality of such clothing. "No dress can be cheaper, nor more convenient, as the wearer may be cool in warm weather and warm in cool weather by putting on undercloaths which will not change the outward dress, Winter or Summer - Besides which it is a dress justly supposed to carry no small terror to the

enemy, who think every such person is a complete marksman."

Originally, the hunting shirt was designed as a substitute for those without uniform coats, not as a uniform in itself. But in a short time it was used almost exclusively around camp to save wear and tear on the uniforms. And, not generally realized, it became the favored dress when the soldiers went into battle. Indeed, it was the only sort of uniform that many of the soldiers owned.

All the shirts were of the same pattern, and made of deer leather, homespun or linen. To distinguish between regiments, they were dyed such colors as yellow, blue, green, purple, brown, black or white.

MAKING THE HUNTING SHIRT

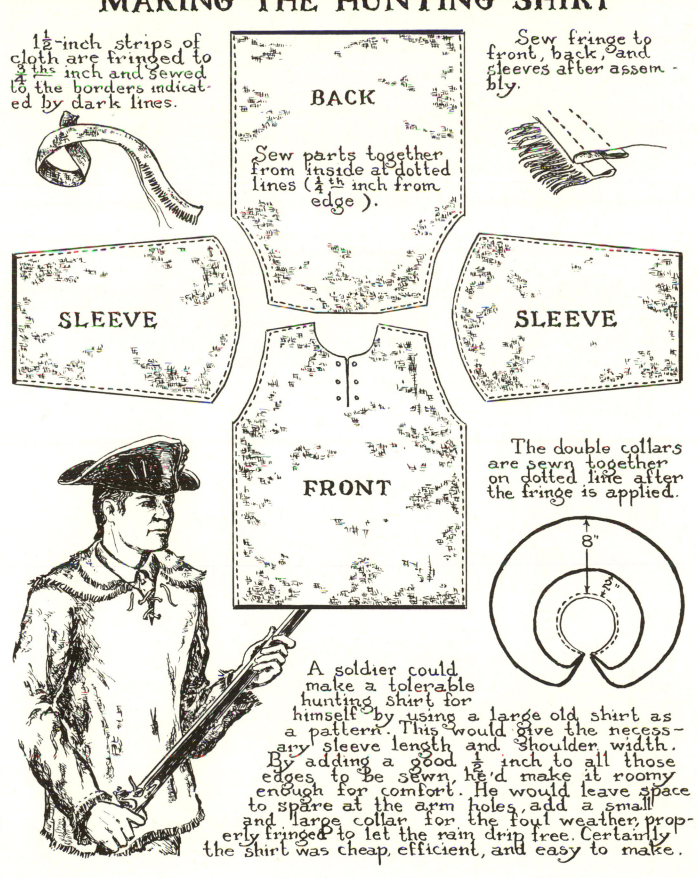

1½-inch strips of cloth are fringed to ¾ths inch and sewed to the borders indicated by dark lines.

BACK

Sew parts together from inside at dotted lines (¼th inch from edge).

Sew fringe to front, back, and sleeves after assembly.

SLEEVE

SLEEVE

FRONT

The double collars are sewn together on dotted line after the fringe is applied.

8"

A soldier could make a tolerable hunting shirt for himself by using a large old shirt as a pattern. This would give the necessary sleeve length and shoulder width. By adding a good ½ inch to all those edges to be sewn, he'd make it roomy enough for comfort. He would leave space to spare at the arm holes, add a small and large collar for the foul weather, properly fringed to let the rain drip free. Certainly the shirt was cheap, efficient, and easy to make.

UNIFORMITY OF UNIFORMS

In addition to hunting shirts, some could boast of a uniform coat. Although brown was considered the official color in 1775, some states had already outfitted their troops in other colors. On the camp parade ground, the many shades and styles of uniforms resembled a patchwork quilt.

With an eye toward better uniformity, Washington issued his General Order of October 2, 1779. The coat was changed to blue with facing

according to the state or region. Therefore the infantry from the New England States, consisting of New Hampshire, Massachusetts, Rhode Island and Connecticut, wore white facing; New York and New Jersey, buff facings; Pennsylvania, Delaware, Maryland and Virginia, red facing; North and South Carolina and Georgia, blue facings with buttonholes edged with narrow white tape.

The breeches and stockings were gradually replaced by the long overalls or leggings. These were fashioned from deer leather, undyed linen or duck. They were shaped to the leg, fastened with four buttons at the ankle and secured by a strap running in front of the heel.

With the first sizable French shipments of coats, breeches and shoes in 1778, whole divisions were finally outfitted with some uniformity. And although the states conformed to the 1779 order in varying degrees, the smart blue uniform was still secondary to the basic problem of covering the Continental soldier's nakedness. In such trying times, orders were more easily written than followed.

CONTINENTAL LIGHT INFANTRYMAN-1780

Pride filled the hearts of all patriots and young ladies cast admiring glances when the Light Infantry Corps marched by. And it was the ambition of every soldier and officer to be counted among their number. Since 1777, young veterans were selected from the various regiments for the honor. They were personally trained by Von Steuben.

Specializing in the difficult, the Light Infantry took both Stony Point and the redoubt at York- town at bayonet point, muskets unloaded. With a detachment of cavalry and riflemen, they marched as the advanced guard for the main army.

New French muskets were part of the well- uniformed and -equipped Corps.

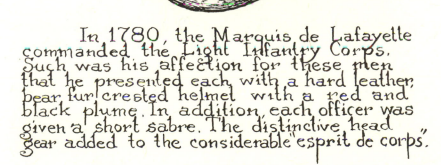

In 1780, the Marquis de Lafayette commanded the Light Infantry Corps. Such was his affection for these men that he presented each with a hard leather, bear fur crested helmet with a red and black plume. In addition, each officer was given a short sabre. The distinctive head gear added to the considerable "esprit de corps".

UNIFORM NOTES

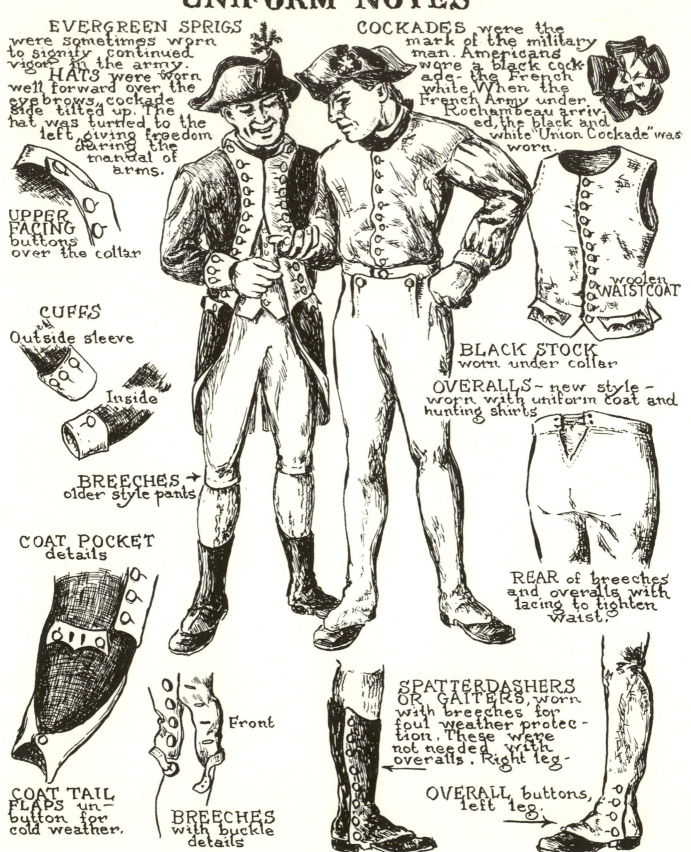

EVERGREEN SPRIGS were sometimes worn to signify continued vigor in the army.

HATS were worn well forward over the eyebrows, cockade side tilted up. The hat was turned to the left giving freedom during the manual of arms.

UPPER FACING buttons over the collar

CUFFS Outside sleeve

Inside

BREECHES → older style pants

COAT POCKET details

COAT TAIL FLAPS unbutton for cold weather.

Front

BREECHES with buckle details

COCKADES were the mark of the military man. Americans wore a black cockade- the French white. When the French Army under Rochambeau arrived, the black and white "Union Cockade" was worn.

woolen **WAISTCOAT**

BLACK STOCK worn under collar

OVERALLS ~ new style ~ worn with uniform coat and hunting shirts

REAR of breeches and overalls with lacing to tighten waist.

SPATTERDASHERS OR GAITERS, worn with breeches for foul weather protection. These were not needed with overalls. Right leg-

OVERALL buttons, left leg.

SOLDIERS' BONE BUTTONS

Yankee thrift found use for most things around the camp, including the lowly meat bone. Bone blanks were first shaved to proper thickness. Then with a carpenter's brace and special bit, buttons were cut. These were covered with cloth and sewn to the uniforms.

By contrast, fine wood-packed buttons were sometimes imported from France for use by the Continental officers. Thin pieces of silver-plated copper or tin were beaten into a form to give a raised design. A paste or cement was applied to the back, and edges bent around the wood backing. The crossed loops of cord or gut were sewn to the uniform. (See below)

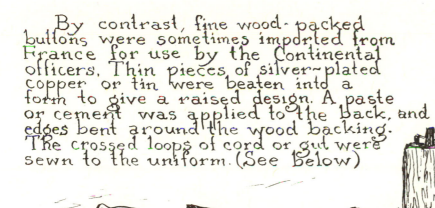

OFFICERS' FRENCH-MADE BUTTONS

Design beaten into mold   Paste applied   Wood back attached

CAST PEWTER BUTTONS

The enlisted men's buttons were crudely cast from pewter or lead. The larger size was for the uniform coats. The smaller sizes were made for the waistcoats.

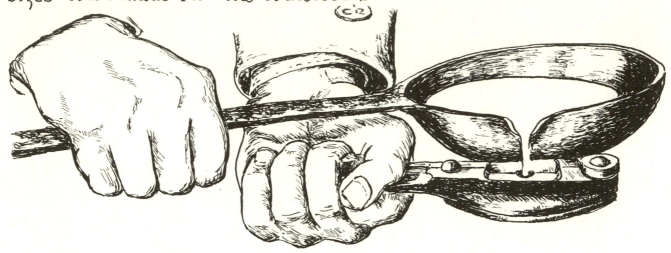

The pewter was heated in a ladle to its molten state. It was then poured into the shank hole to fill the button cavity. Pre-heating the mold helped the metal to flow into all parts of the button form.

When the metal had cooled to a solid state, the handles were opened and the casting removed.

The excess metal was removed with nippers and remelted. The button was finished by filing and polishing.

The small size of the mold was carried handily in the soldiers' packs. Many buttons were camp-made.

CONTINENTAL BUTTON DESIGNS

The officers' fine wood-backed buttons, with the exception of style 1, bore the same raised design as the soldiers' pewter buttons.

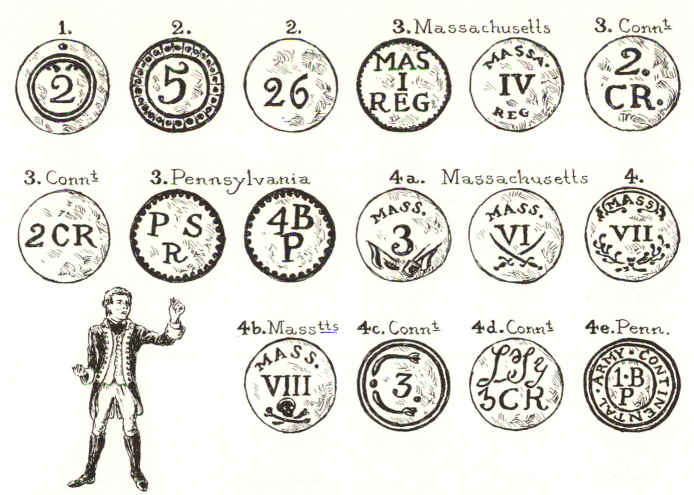

1.   2.   2.   3. Massachusetts   3. Conn.ᵗ

2   5   26   MAS I REG   MASSA. IV REG   2. CR.

3. Conn.ᵗ   3. Pennsylvania   4a. Massachusetts   4.

2CR   PSR   4BP   MASS. 3   MASS. VI   MASS VII

4b. Masstts   4c. Conn.ᵗ   4d. Conn.ᵗ   4e. Penn.

MASS. VIII   3   L.I. 3CR   ARMY·CONTINENTAL 1·B P

1. NUMERALS – FRENCH MODEL 1762
Imported for Continental officer.

2. NUMERALS – REGIMENTAL
Originated with the General Orders of November 13, 1775 for the twenty-seven Continental regiments.

3. NUMERALS & STATE NAMES 1777–1783
States were added to regimental numbers.

4. NUMERALS WITH SPECIAL DESIGNS
a. War trophy of flags & drum.
b. Skull & cross bones of the "Bloody 8th."
c. Two dolphins in form of "C" for Connecticut in honor of French Dauphin, born in 1781.
d. Light Infantry, 3rd Connecticut Regiment.
e. "B" is for "Battalion" – synonymous for "Regiment".

5. Rhode Is.  **5. New York**  **5. New Jersey**  **5. Delaware**  **5. Maryland**

6a.  **6b.**  **7.**  **7.**  **8.**

9a.  **9b.**  **9c.**  **10.** 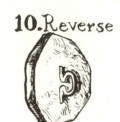 **10. Reverse**

5. STATE WITHOUT NUMERALS

6. WITHOUT STATE OR NUMERALS

a. Regiment raised in Boston after British evacuation, 1776. Inimica Tyrannis = hostile to tyrants.
b. Bucks Of America - A Negro corps raised in New England.

7. U.S.A. BUTTONS 1777-1782

The most common type of Continental button used by units not connected with state regiments.

8. NAVY

9. ARTILLERY CORPS

Buttons were usually bronze instead of pewter.
a. Cohorn mortar.
b. Field cannon with British Union flag - indicates early use, perhaps 1776.
c. Two cannon and trophy of flags.

10. NON-MILITARY BUTTONS

Widely used where military buttons not available. These flat, solid buttons were plain or hand engraved. Usually of brass, they had metal loop shanks brazed on the backs.

FOOT WEAR

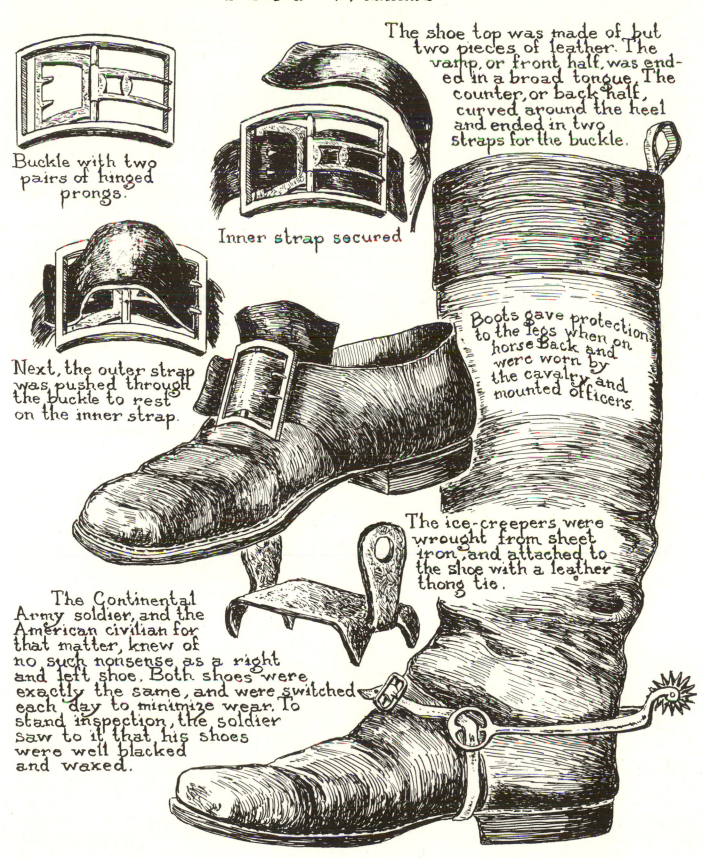

Buckle with two pairs of hinged prongs.

Inner strap secured

The shoe top was made of but two pieces of leather. The vamp, or front half, was ended in a broad tongue. The counter, or back half, curved around the heel and ended in two straps for the buckle.

Next, the outer strap was pushed through the buckle to rest on the inner strap.

Boots gave protection to the legs when on horse back and were worn by the cavalry and mounted officers.

The ice-creepers were wrought from sheet iron, and attached to the shoe with a leather thong tie.

The Continental Army soldier, and the American civilian for that matter, knew of no such nonsense as a right and left shoe. Both shoes were exactly the same, and were switched each day to minimize wear. To stand inspection, the soldier saw to it that his shoes were well blacked and waxed.

MUSKETS USED BY THE CONTINENTALS

Speed of firing—that was the thing! Camp drills pounded this into the infantry-man until he could load and shoot his musket every 15 seconds. In actual combat, the greater the hail of bullets into the close-packed ranks of the enemy, the nearer was victory. Careful aiming in the short distance between two massed armies was not only un-necessary but time-consuming.

The smooth bore musket was certainly the gun of choice. With-out rifling, a ball could be quickly rammed down the bore without need-ing the snug fit that rifle patches gave. Maximum accuracy was but 100 yards, and was all the distance necessary to lay down a heavy pattern of volley firing. Further, when meeting the enemy charge the mus-ket's bayonet was a must in the hand-to-hand fighting that followed.

MILITIAMAN'S FOWLER

Every colonist was required to own a musket when serving in the state militia. This semi-military gun could pass muster inspection and serve as a hunting piece as well. Unfortunately, they were rarely fitted with bayonets. Frequently, the musket was a thrifty mixture of parts from worn-out weapons.

BROWN BESS MUSKET

This standard British musket was favored by the Continentals early in the war. When hostilities began, each state Committee of Safety contracted with local gun-smiths to reproduce this firearm to augment those already in the colonies. As with the Brown Bess, the barrel was secured to the stock by pins and carried the typical brass fittings—other-wise known as "furniture".

FRENCH MUSKET

The muskets of America's new ally found increasing favor as the war continued. Most of the muskets were fitted with iron rather than brass furniture. The characteristic bands that bound the barrel could be slipped off and the barrel removed for easier cleaning. In contrast to the British "goose neck" cock the French cock was reinforced to spare it from the constant battering of the flint against the frizzen.

THE LOCK=WORK HORSE OF THE MUSKET

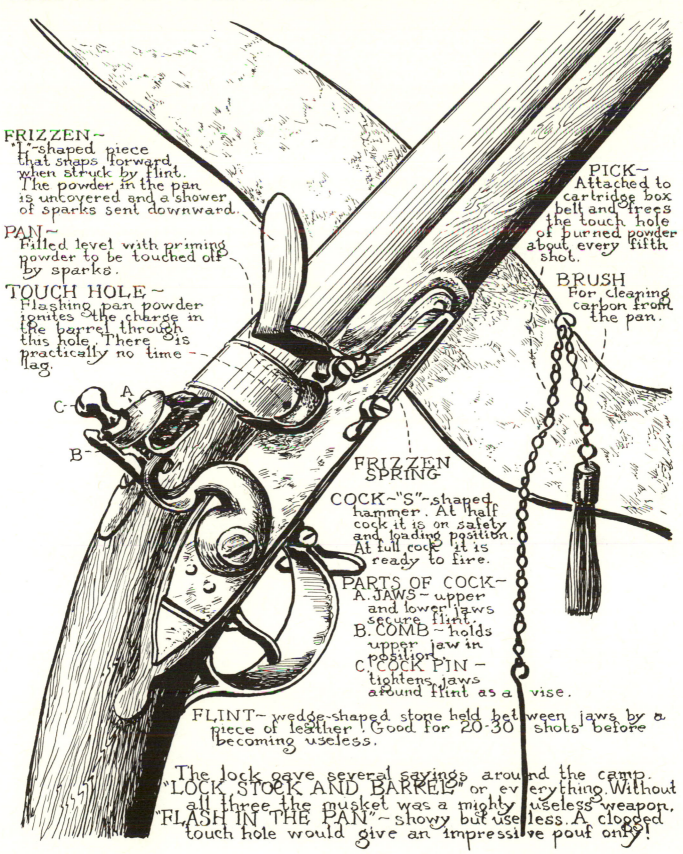

FRIZZEN~
"L"~shaped piece that snaps forward when struck by flint. The powder in the pan is uncovered and a shower of sparks sent downward.

PAN ~
Filled level with priming powder to be touched off by sparks.

TOUCH HOLE ~
Flashing pan powder ignites the charge in the barrel through this hole. There is practically no time lag.

PICK~
Attached to cartridge box belt and frees the touch hole of burned powder about every fifth shot.

BRUSH
For cleaning carbon from the pan.

FRIZZEN SPRING

COCK~"S"~shaped hammer. At half cock it is on safety and loading position. At full cock it is ready to fire.

PARTS OF COCK~
A.JAWS~ upper and lower jaws secure flint.
B. COMB~ holds upper jaw in position.
C.COCK PIN — tightens jaws around flint as a vise.

FLINT~ wedge-shaped stone held between jaws by a piece of leather. Good for 20-30 shots before becoming useless.

The lock gave several sayings around the camp. "LOCK, STOCK AND BARREL" or everything. Without all three the musket was a mighty useless weapon. "FLASH IN THE PAN"~ showy but useless. A clogged touch hole would give an impressive pouf only!

ROLL THOSE CARTRIDGES!

Certainly the proper preparation of cartridges was an important camp duty. In the heat of battle, loading the musket from a powder horn could be a nerve-racking business. Therefore a ready-made tube of measured powder and ball was a blessing to the hard-pressed soldier.

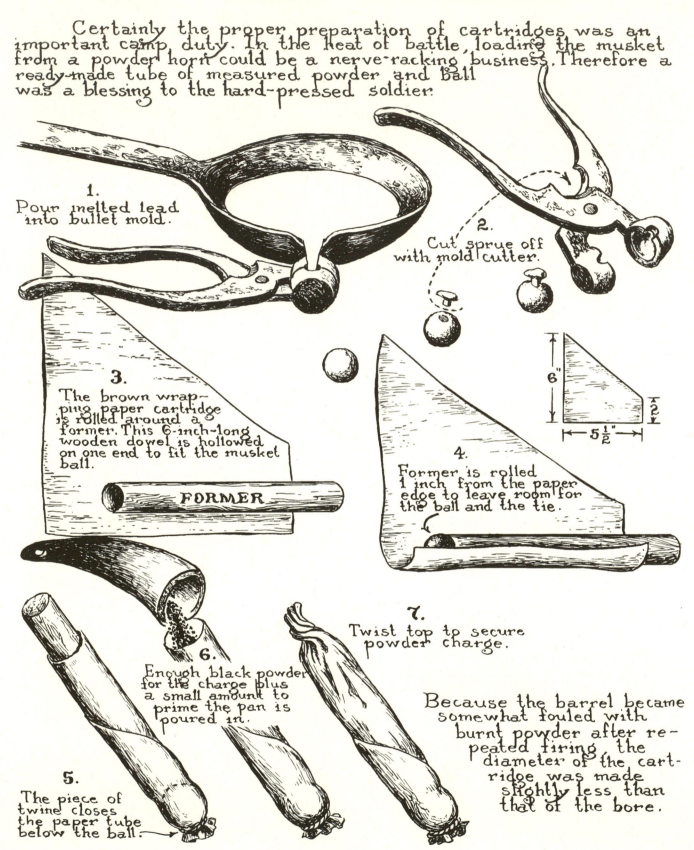

1. Pour melted lead into bullet mold.

2. Cut sprue off with mold cutter.

3. The brown wrapping paper cartridge is rolled around a former. This 6-inch-long wooden dowel is hollowed on one end to fit the musket ball.

FORMER

4. Former is rolled 1 inch from the paper edge to leave room for the ball and the tie.

6"

5 1/2"

5. The piece of twine closes the paper tube below the ball.

6. Enough black powder for the charge plus a small amount to prime the pan is poured in.

7. Twist top to secure powder charge.

Because the barrel became somewhat fouled with burnt powder after repeated firing, the diameter of the cartridge was made slightly less than that of the bore.

22

CARTRIDGE BOXES

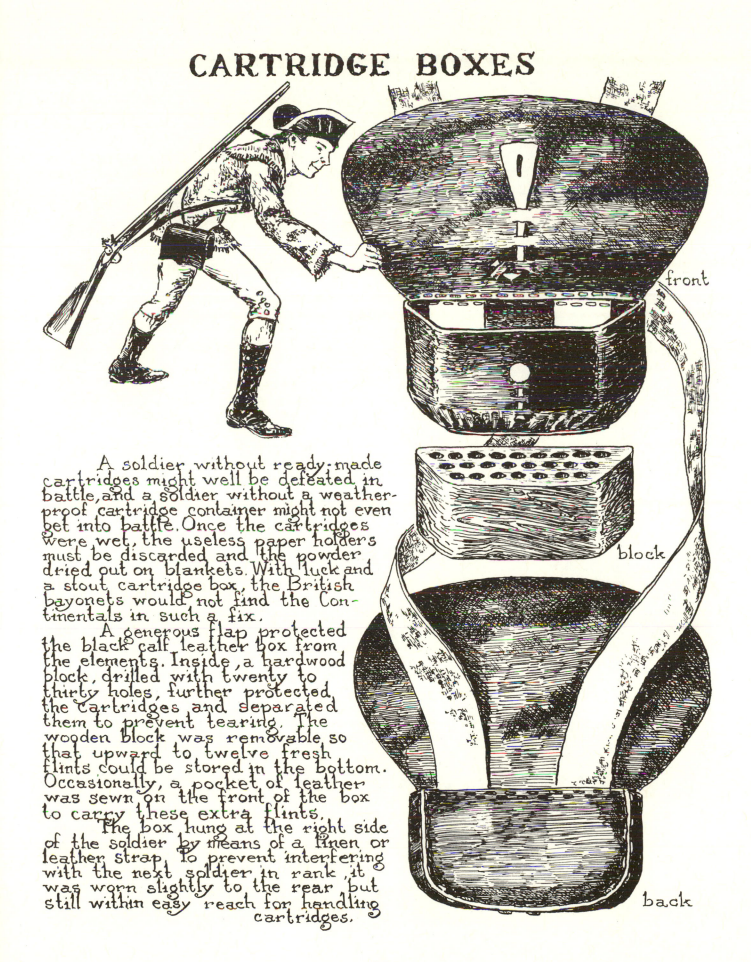

front

block

back

A soldier without ready-made cartridges might well be defeated in battle, and a soldier without a weather-proof cartridge container might not even get into battle. Once the cartridges were wet, the useless paper holders must be discarded and the powder dried out on blankets. With luck and a stout cartridge box, the British bayonets would not find the Continentals in such a fix.

A generous flap protected the black calf leather box from the elements. Inside, a hardwood block, drilled with twenty to thirty holes, further protected the cartridges and separated them to prevent tearing. The wooden block was removable so that upward to twelve fresh flints could be stored in the bottom. Occasionally, a pocket of leather was sewn on the front of the box to carry these extra flints.

The box hung at the right side of the soldier by means of a linen or leather strap. To prevent interfering with the next soldier in rank, it was worn slightly to the rear but still within easy reach for handling cartridges.

23

WAIST CARTRIDGE BOX

The waist cartridge box was worn by special troops such as the Light Infantry, and the cavalry. It was smaller than the shoulder box and was worn at the front of the waist belt.

TIN CANNISTER

The scarcity of good water-proof cartridge boxes gave birth to an admirable substitute. The tin cannister could carry thirty-six cartridges in layers of four, quite safe from the rain. Three tin loops, soldered to the sides and bottom, held a shoulder belt a full inch and a half wide.

Not only was the box light to carry and free from dampness, it was fireproof as well. The hinged cover opened against part of the belt. After a cartridge was removed, it would fall shut and prevent ignition of the remaining cartridges.

The tin was japanned or painted to prevent rusting.

CAMP NEEDS CHANGE THE BULLET

MUTILATED MUSKET BALLS

Although outlawed by both British and Americans, they were occasionally made in both camps. They would fragment or tear into the unfortunate target.

Partially halved

With nail

Partially quartered

DICE

FISH LINE SINKERS

NET SINKERS

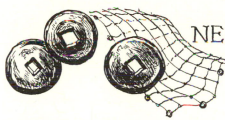

CHEWED BULLET

A wounded soldier had the small comfort of a ration of rum and a bullet to chew during surgery.

BUTTON

Cloth-covered round or "a bit flattened" ball made a makeshift button.

HALF BULLET

½-ounce weight. Occasionally used as a farthing for coined money was just another camp scarcity.

UNIFORM WEIGHT

Holds hem down.

ONE OUNCE

Weight is flattened to prevent rolling.

FLINT SHEATH

Thin lead sheet holds flint snugly between jaws of the cock.

LEAD PENCILS

CHILD'S BUZZER

Teeth set alternately to right and left to produce a humming or buzzing noise. A loop of stout twine drives it.

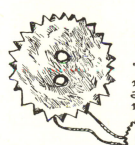

THE SILVER BULLET
OCTOBER 10, 1777

The rider reined in his lathered horse and glared down at the group of men who had challenged him. There was no time for dallying about New Windsor, for the message he carried from the British General Henry Clinton was already two days delayed. All haste must be made to deliver it to General Burgoyne, presently stalled before the Americans along the upper Hudson River. He must know that Clinton had gobbled up the rebel forts of Clinton and Montgomery, and was continuing the diversion northward. Certainly there could be few of the scattered American forces about to bring grief to his errand.

As a safeguard, although it seemed unnecessary, the note had been written on tissue paper and folded into a hollow silver bullet. If he were to fall into unfriendly hands, the evidence need only be swallowed. But for the present, he must cover the miles. Somewhat impatiently he said "I am a friend, and wish to see General Clinton." One look at the silver bullet and the General would speed him on his way.

Although the British messenger did not know it, there was an American general by the name of George Clinton. He had escaped while commanding the fallen forts, and was now gathering his disordered army at this place. When confronted by the wrong General Clinton, the rider turned a sickly shade and groaned "I am lost!" And that he was! In desperation he popped the silver container with its message into his mouth and gulped it down. A tartar emetic changed the direction of the bullet, but on its reappearance he once again managed to swallow it. Clinton's patience was wearing thin. The visitor was given the choice of another emetic or being strung on a tree and having the bullet removed by a different route with a surgeon's knife.

The choice was not a difficult one to make. Down went the emetic and up came the bullet. The hollow elliptical halves separated, for one half fitted on the narrow shoulder of the other. Convicted by such evidence, the spy was hung high in an apple tree in nearby Kingston. The British had pushed their invasion to that town and were setting the torch to it. So it was that the enemy had their spy returned in exchange for a most unusual bullet.

BAYONETS

Early in the Revolution, American blacksmiths patterned the bayonet after the British. When the French entered the conflict, the pattern was changed in favor of the new allies. Pattern or not, it was no easy chore to fit a socket to the hodge-podge of barrels in the Continental Army.

All bayonets locked in place to the right of the barrel (on the same side as the lock) out of the way for loading and firing.

BRITISH BAYONET

1. Blade 16 inches long.
2. Blade square at base.
3. Rear reinforcing band with notch to allow entry of barrel stud.
4. Zig-zag ⌐ slot in socket to lock against barrel stud.

FRENCH BAYONETS

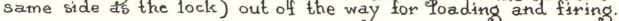

1. Blade 14-14½ inches long.
2. Blade curved at base.
3. Slotted sockets vary according to the year first made.

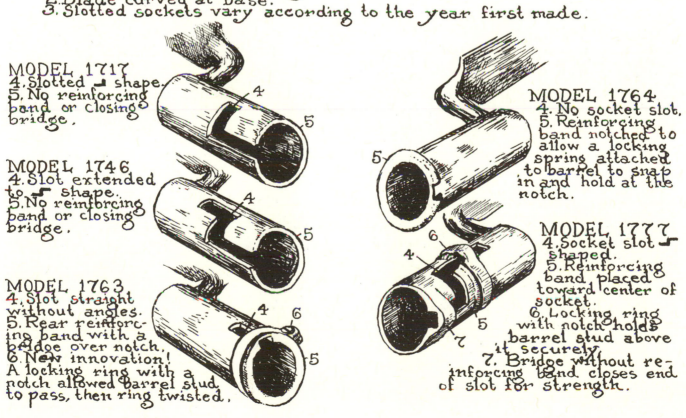

MODEL 1717
4. Slotted ⌐ shape.
5. No reinforcing band or closing bridge.

MODEL 1746
4. Slot extended to ⌐ shape.
5. No reinforcing band or closing bridge.

MODEL 1763
4. Slot straight without angles.
5. Rear reinforcing band with a bridge over notch.
6. New innovation! A locking ring with a notch allowed barrel stud to pass, then ring twisted.

MODEL 1764
4. No socket slot.
5. Reinforcing band notched to allow a locking spring attached to barrel to snap in and hold at the notch.

MODEL 1777
4. Socket slot ⌐ shaped.
5. Reinforcing band placed toward center of socket.
6. Locking ring with notch holds barrel stud above it securely.
7. Bridge without reinforcing band closes end of slot for strength.

DRILL MASTER STEUBEN

Frederick William Augustus Henry Ferdinand, Baron von Steuben shook off sleep at three in the morning, read for a spell with a pipeful of tobacco, then was ready for his day after a hot cup of coffee. There was much to do, for the American camp at Valley Forge had known only the variety of haphazard drills from the scattered militia training grounds.

By six in the morning, Steuben was putting squads of ten to twelve soldiers through their paces. Once these smaller units had mastered Steuben's simplified manual of arms and field maneuvers, the tireless, bombastic newcomer moved on to a platoon, to a company, and then to the regiments, until the entire army moved as one under unified commands.

When exasperation replaced patience, the stout, balding and rather large-nosed German exploded in a tirade of swearing in his native tongue, then in French, then in a tumble of both. Running out of choice epithets, he would call to an aide to come and swear for him in English. As one onlooker reported, "a good-natured smile went through the ranks and at last the maneuver was properly performed."

Meanwhile, fellow officers looked on in amazement, unaware that they were witnessing a revolution within a revolution. There was a Lieutenant General, personally working with the rank and file, showing an obvious concern and deep regard for the men while maintaining strict discipline. The officers became less aloof, and the morale of the ragged, underfed, and underpaid troops rose to a new high.

The officers were not forgotten. After drilling the soldiers until six in the evening, Steuben held special classes on maneuvering and commands for the adjutants. Once he invited a number of young officers to a sumptuous camp banquet of tough beefsteaks, potatoes, and a dessert of hickory nuts. None were to be admitted with a whole pair of breeches, and no one failed to qualify!

Steuben's infectious enthusiasm for precision movements gave the Continental Army a new measure of confidence. With backs stiffened by discipline and respect for authority, the rejuvenated rebels were ready to meet the British on equal terms.

LOADING AND FIRING THE MUSKET

Commands for training the troops in camp – by Von Steuben

1. HALF COCK FIRELOCK.

2. HANDLE CARTRIDGE.
Top is bitten off and covered with the thumb.

3. PRIME.
Shake powder into pan.

4. SHUT PAN.

5. CHARGE WITH CARTRIDGE.

6. DRAW RAMROD.

7. RAM DOWN CARTRIDGE.

8. RETURN RAMROD. and immediately bring to shoulder position.

9. SHOULDER FIRELOCK. Loaded and ready.

10. POISE FIRELOCK.
11. COCK FIRELOCK.

12. TAKE AIM.
13. FIRE!

Immediately bring musket to first position ready for half cock.

RIFLEMAN

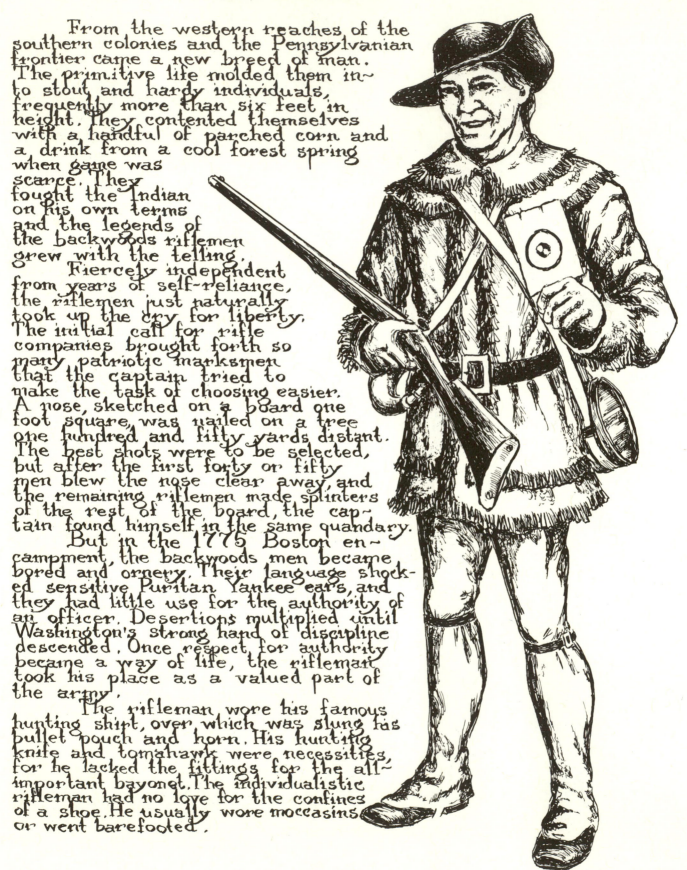

From the western reaches of the southern colonies and the Pennsylvanian frontier came a new breed of man. The primitive life molded them into stout and hardy individuals, frequently more than six feet in height. They contented themselves with a handful of parched corn and a drink from a cool forest spring when game was scarce. They fought the Indian on his own terms and the legends of the backwoods riflemen grew with the telling.

Fiercely independent from years of self-reliance, the riflemen just naturally took up the cry for liberty. The initial call for rifle companies brought forth so many patriotic marksmen that the captain tried to make the task of choosing easier. A nose, sketched on a board one foot square, was nailed on a tree one hundred and fifty yards distant. The best shots were to be selected, but after the first forty or fifty men blew the nose clear away, and the remaining riflemen made splinters of the rest of the board, the captain found himself in the same quandary.

But in the 1775 Boston encampment, the backwoods men became bored and ornery. Their language shocked sensitive Puritan Yankee ears, and they had little use for the authority of an officer. Desertions multiplied until Washington's strong hand of discipline descended. Once respect for authority became a way of life, the rifleman took his place as a valued part of the army.

The rifleman wore his famous hunting shirt, over which was slung his bullet pouch and horn. His hunting knife and tomahawk were necessities, for he lacked the fittings for the all-important bayonet. The individualistic rifleman had no love for the confines of a shoe. He usually wore moccasins or went barefooted.

THE RIFLE - FACTS AND FABLES

There are many who believe the Americans fought Indian fashion behind trees and split-rail fences, knocking down the brightly uniformed British like a row of ten pins. Other than the British retreat from Lexington and Concord and the Kings Mountain battle, it just wasn't so! Perhaps the storied American rifle would have played a more important role if woodland skirmishing had been the rule.

The rifleman found himself badly short-changed by the slow loading of his piece, and the fact that he had no means of attaching a bayonet to defend himself when caught in the act of loading. It would be a distressing situation indeed to find a rush of Redcoats bearing down, bayonets aslant, with but a single rifle load between him and eternity.

But the rifle, by virtue of its spiraled grooves, could boast of great accuracy. With a keen eye behind the sights, a target at 250 to 300 yards was in danger of being perforated. Therefore the riflemen found a valued place in the Continental Army as scouts, snipers and skirmishers when supported by musket-bearing troops. The British soldier had a healthy respect for the sharpshooter who might be training his "Widow and Orphan Maker" on him at any moment.

PENNSYLVANIA OR KENTUCKY RIFLE

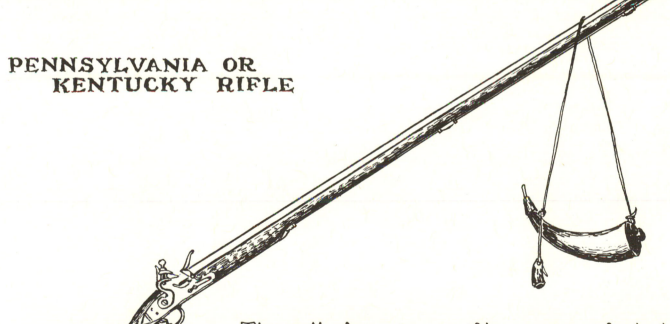

This all-American rifle was perfected by the Pennsylvania gunsmiths and proved on the Kentucky frontier and the Revolutionary battlegrounds. Each gun was as individual as the man who carried it, but all were beautifully balanced and deadly accurate.

The simple brass patch box held the greased cloth patches that gave a tight fit to the ball in the rifled barrel. The handsome brass and silver inlays usually associated with the rifle were added in the post-Revolutionary period.

LOADING THE RIFLE

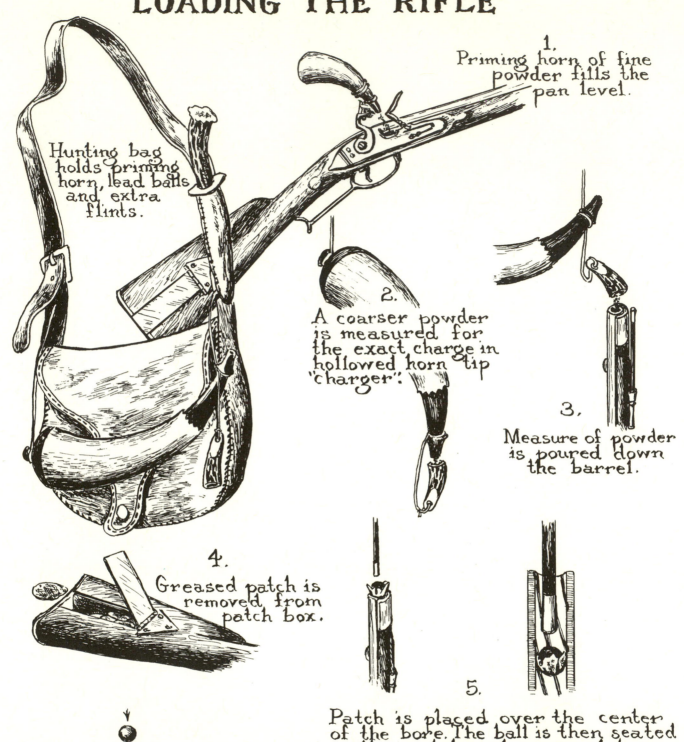

1. Priming horn of fine powder fills the pan level.

Hunting bag holds priming horn, lead balls and extra flints.

2. A coarser powder is measured for the exact charge in hollowed horn tip "charger".

3. Measure of powder is poured down the barrel.

4. Greased patch is removed from patch box.

5. Patch is placed over the center of the bore. The ball is then seated on the patch and rammed home.

4. & 5. To speed the slow loading, a board with several bored holes was sometimes used. A hole, containing a patched ball, was placed over the bore. Then the ball was rammed in.

POWDER HORNS

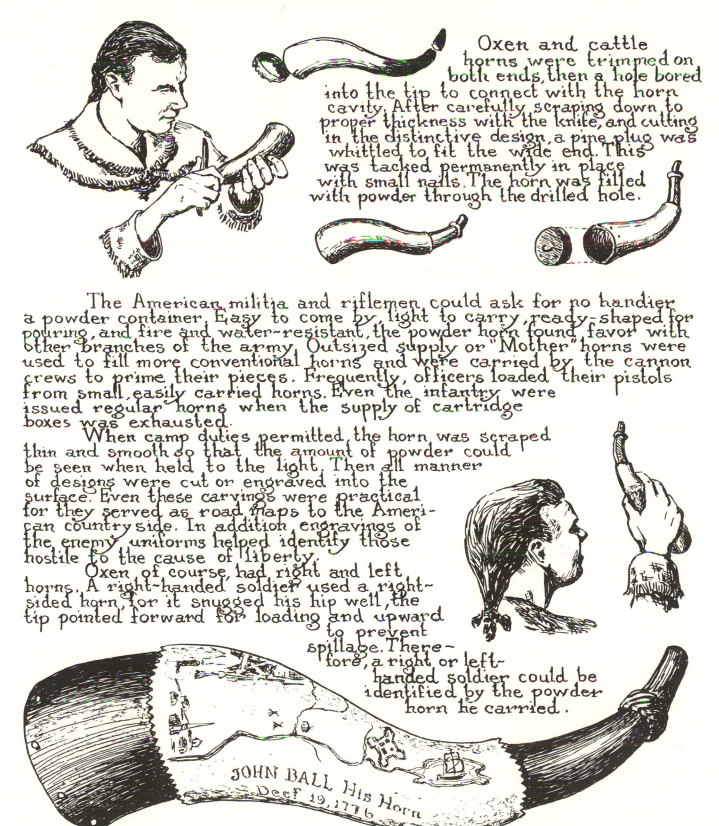

Oxen and cattle horns were trimmed on both ends, then a hole bored into the tip to connect with the horn cavity. After carefully scraping down to proper thickness with the knife, and cutting in the distinctive design, a pine plug was whittled to fit the wide end. This was tacked permanently in place with small nails. The horn was filled with powder through the drilled hole.

The American militia and riflemen could ask for no handier a powder container. Easy to come by, light to carry, ready-shaped for pouring, and fire and water-resistant, the powder horn found favor with other branches of the army. Outsized supply or "Mother" horns were used to fill more conventional horns and were carried by the cannon crews to prime their pieces. Frequently, officers loaded their pistols from small, easily carried horns. Even the infantry were issued regular horns when the supply of cartridge boxes was exhausted.

When camp duties permitted, the horn was scraped thin and smooth so that the amount of powder could be seen when held to the light. Then all manner of designs were cut or engraved into the surface. Even these carvings were practical for they served as road maps to the American countryside. In addition, engravings of the enemy uniforms helped identify those hostile to the cause of liberty.

Oxen, of course, had right and left horns. A right-handed soldier used a right-sided horn, for it snugged his hip well, the tip pointed forward for loading and upward to prevent spillage. Therefore, a right or left-handed soldier could be identified by the powder horn he carried.

JOHN BALL His Horn
Dec. 19, 1776

TOMAHAWK, BELT AX, OR IRON TRADE AX

A sheet of hot iron was folded around an iron bar to make the eye. The blade was welded by hammering.

Steel was scarce; therefore a steel wedge was often welded in to make a hard cutting edge.

The weld line identifies a hand-wrought piece.

Poll

Eye →

Bit

Handle or Helve ~ always straight

The Army issued one of these tomahawks to every six-man cooking detail. This important camp tool served as a potent weapon as well. American riflemen had no attachment for bayonets, and therefore relied on this side arm. Frequently the militia carried the tomahawk with or without a bayonet.

TOMAHAWK TYPES

ROUND OR OVAL EYE

 Round   Oval   Flat Poll

Easily made or repaired by the camp blacksmith these tomahawks were favorites in the Continental Army. And they were certainly not strangers in the Indian or enemy camp, for the Royal Highland Regiment (Black Watch) and regiments of the British Light Infantry carried them in the Revolution.

Styled after the large felling ax, the oval eye tomahawks were the earliest; the oval eye did not appear until the early 1700's.

SPIKE POLE

Few were seen around the Revolutionary camp~grounds, for the spike had proved downright unhandy. In battle, the soldier or Indian could be his own victim when he reached for his tomahawk. Therefore, the spike was gradually shortened until it had entirely disappeared by the end    of the 1700's.

PIPE TOMAHAWK

Let the white soldier seek contentment from his fragile clay pipe! This multipurpose side arm served the Indian well around his encampment, was deadly on the warpath, gave the braves keen competition in tomahawk throwing, then the relaxation of a smoke around the camp fire.

The iron tomahawk, with its welded bowl, was an instant success when introduced in the early 1700's. The cast brass version appeared around 1750.

SPONTOON~SHAPED TOMAHAWK

The Indian nations frowned on these poorly balanced and unwieldly side arms since their introduction in the early 1700's. They were styled after the spear-shaped spontoon carried by commissioned officers as a symbol of rank.

CARRYING & THROWING THE TOMAHAWK

1. Take five steps from target. At this distance of ten feet, the tomahawk makes two turns and strikes.

2. Hold the butt end of the handle in the middle of the palm of the hand.

3. Keep feet apart with weight of body resting on the right leg.

4. Fix eyes on target— not the tomahawk.

5. Throw tomahawk forward smartly.

6. Do not jerk the handle back when throwing. This would brand you as a namby-pamby with unmistakable lady-like qualities.

A. The private of the 11th Regiment of Virginia carries his tomahawk in a belt loop.

B. The militiaman wears a shoulder belt with a double frog for his tomahawk and bayonet.

36

SHEATH OR BELT KNIVES

RIFLE KNIFE – Rifle patches were wrapped about the ball to seat it snugly against the rifled grooves in the barrel. To cut these greased patches of cloth, the riflemen used this small handy knife which was carried in the rifle bag or by a sheath attached to the bag or its strap.

Handles were antler, cow horn or wood – blade length 3 or 4 inches.

DAGGER – This rare weapon was as individual as the officer who carried it, for there were no regulations to govern the design. Generally a guard was present, blade double-edged and 6 inches long.

HUNTING, FIGHTING OR SCALPING KNIFE – This knife was a trademark of the frontiersmen and riflemen. They were carried in a leather belt sheath.

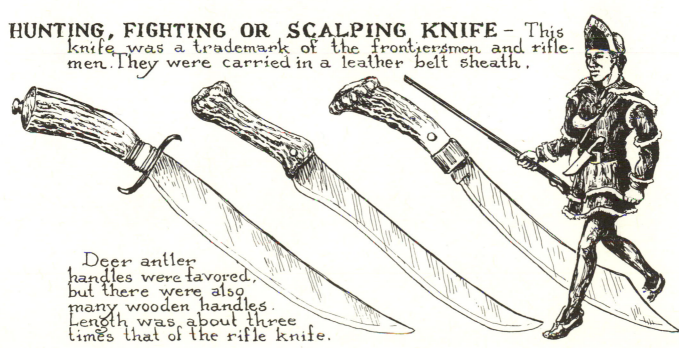

Deer antler handles were favored, but there were also many wooden handles. Length was about three times that of the rifle knife.

CAMP-MADE RIFLEMAN'S HUNTING KNIFE

Ordinarily, the hunting knife was made by the home town blacksmith. After heating a bar of steel red-hot, he would hammer out the design on his anvil. But give a rifleman an old cross cut saw blade, a few simple tools, and a spare moment away from his camp chores, and he'd have himself a fine hunting knife in short order.

A penciled outline of the future weapon ① was struck smartly with a cold chisel.

If lucky enough to have the use of a vise ② the outline was moved repeatedly along the jaws of the vise as the dents were made. The piece could then be broken along the dents by striking it with a hammer.

The edges were smoothed on a grindstone ③, care being taken to dip the metal in water frequently. The temper would be lost if the steel turned blue or dark in color. Only the third of the blade nearest the cutting edge was gently beveled, the last $\frac{1}{4}$th inch ④ ground into a rounded bevel. Care again was taken not to overheat! The handle section was detempered by burying the blade ⑤, leaving the exposed tang upright. A fire was built about it, and when the metal was red-hot, two

$\frac{1}{4}$th inch

holes were made with a steel punch or nail. Or the metal was soft enough to drill after cooling to the air. There was no need to re-temper the tang. The handle ⑥ was made from a close-grained wood such as apple, hickory or maple. Cut slightly larger than the metal it was shaped down once the handle was screwed ⑦ or riveted in place.

If a guard was de-sired, a pierced piece of brass was slipped on the tang to rest against the blade. ⑧

POCKET KNIVES

JACK KNIFE — This constant companion of the American soldier was always ready to whittle wooden camp ware, engrave a powder horn, or hack at a tough piece of Army beef. Some states, as New Hampshire, New York, and Massachusetts thought so highly of the pocket knife that they required their militia to carry one.

Jack knives were always single-bladed. Folded length was 4-7 inches.

PEN KNIFE — There were always dispatches or letters home to be written. This little knife served to cut new quill pens or sharpen old ones.

Single-bladed – 3 inches when folded.

Gen.ᵗ Washington's pen knife.

FORK POCKET KNIFE —

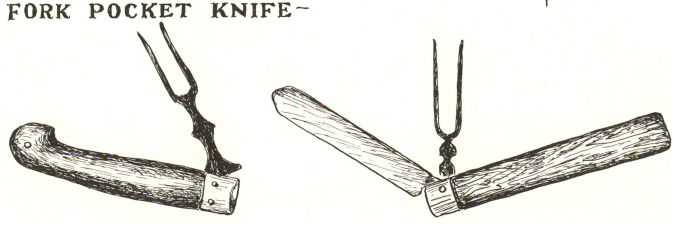

CAVALRY

The heavy cavalry of Europe, made up of large men riding large horses, was used in the battle line to charge infantry or other cavalry units. But in the rugged countryside of America, only light cavalry was found in the British and American camps. These light men, on swift horses for mounted or dismounted service, were known as dragoons. In this dual role, they carried carbines as well as sabers and pistols.

The mobility and speed of the light dragoons allowed them to spy out enemy movements, gallop from forest cover to fall on British convoys and attack enemy forage parties. At camp, patrols of horsemen patrolled the outskirts to discourage deserters or were posted at advanced positions to prevent a surprise attack. When on the march, they joined the light infantry as an advanced guard. In battle, their close cooperation with the infantry often meant the difference between victory or defeat.

But the cavalry fared as badly in their supply of weapons as did the rest of the army. Lacking carbines, they were unable to protect their own camps from attack. Therefore Steuben, in 1780, suggested an interesting marriage between the cavalry and the infantry. The mounted dragoons could now carry out their outpost work under the protection of the foot soldiers as dismounted dragoons. The new regiments were called "legions".

Washington's Order of 1779 directed that the light dragoons wear blue coats faced and lined with white, with white buttons.

CAVALRY HELMETS

Forage Cap

Virginia Light Dragoons

Jockey Cap with fox tail

Bear fur-horse hair-ribbon

Leather cap with brass trim

French brass helmet

These highly decorative helmets were basically for protection. The black japanned boiled leather helmets and the later imported French brass hats could absorb punishment from a saber slash. The brass mountings and cloth or leather turban guarded the sides, and the thick bear fur or flowing horse hair crests warded off blows from the top or the back of the neck.

When not on camp parade, the horse hair crests were braided to prevent snarling.

EQUIPPING THE CAVALRY

Ideally, the cavalry recruit was given a stock, one cap, one comb, one pair of breeches, two pair of stockings, two pair of gaiters, three pair of shoes, one pair of buckles, a spear, and a cartridge box. In addition, each mounted man was to receive a pair of boots, a saddle, a halter, a curry comb, a horse brush, saddle bags, a picket cord and a pack saddle. But the poverty of the Continental Army extended to the cavalry, a branch expensive to equip and maintain. Horses were costly and saddles scarce. In 1778, Washington replied to an urgent appeal from Moylan's Light Dragoons that swords, pistols, and carbines were unobtainable. As late as 1782, the southern cavalry had no cartridge boxes, the few pistols were unfit for use, and one third of the men had no scabbards.

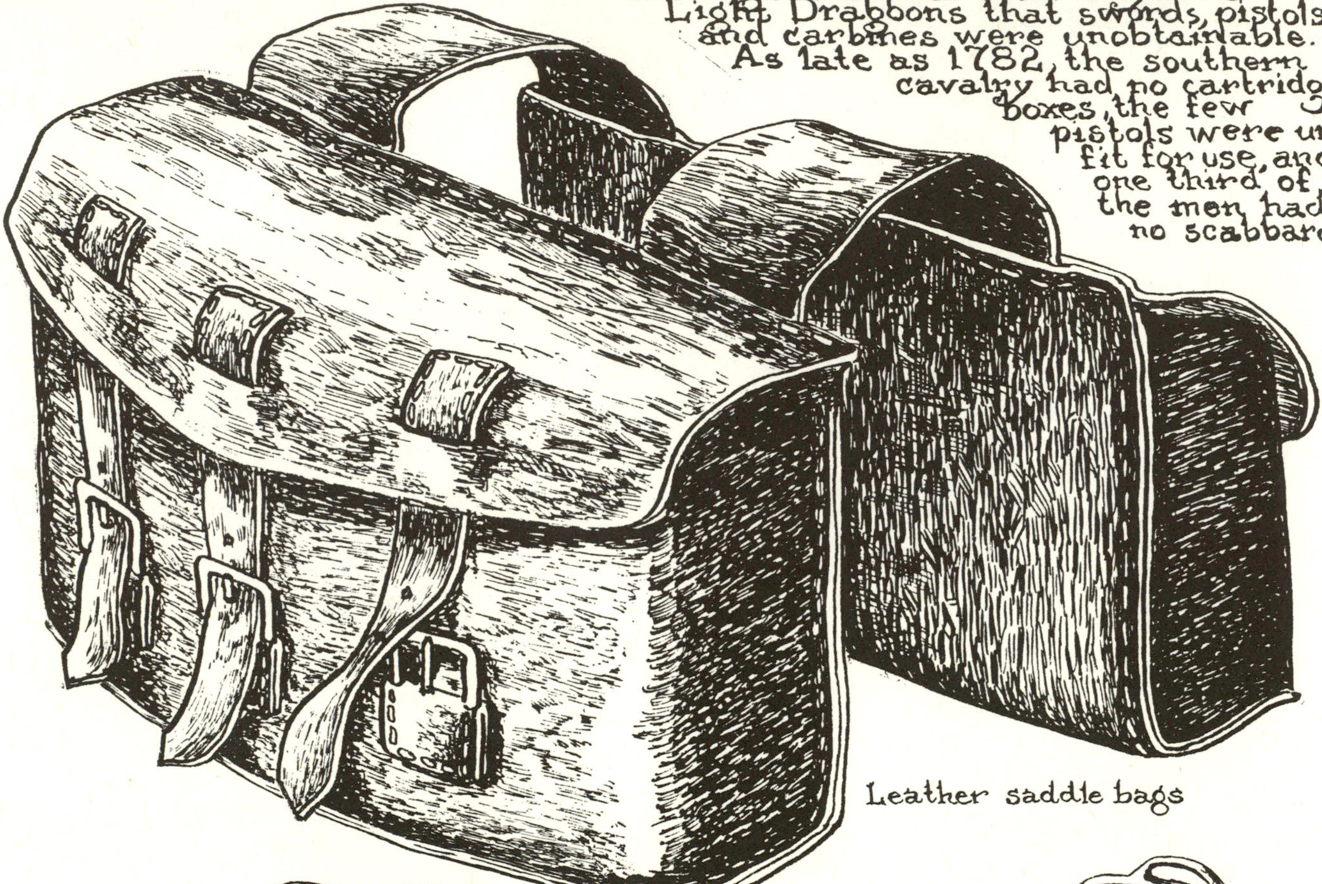

Leather saddle bags

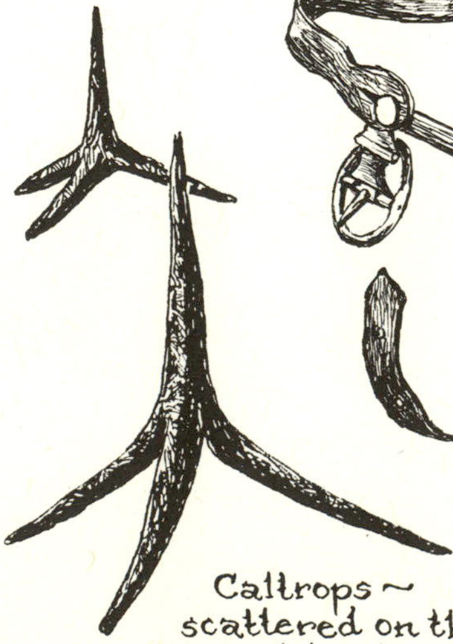

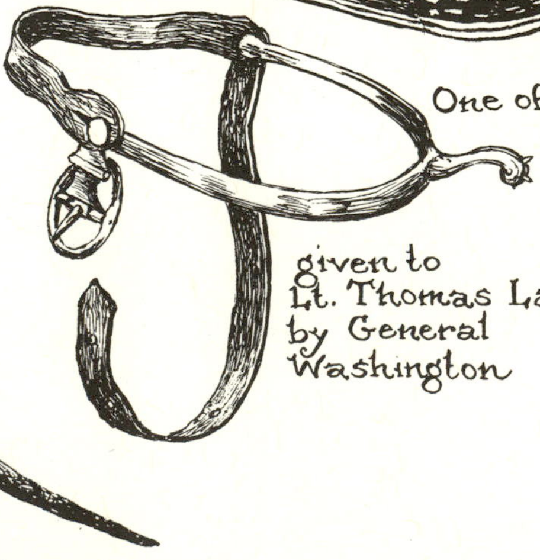

One of a pair of silver spurs ~ given to Lt. Thomas Lamb by General Washington

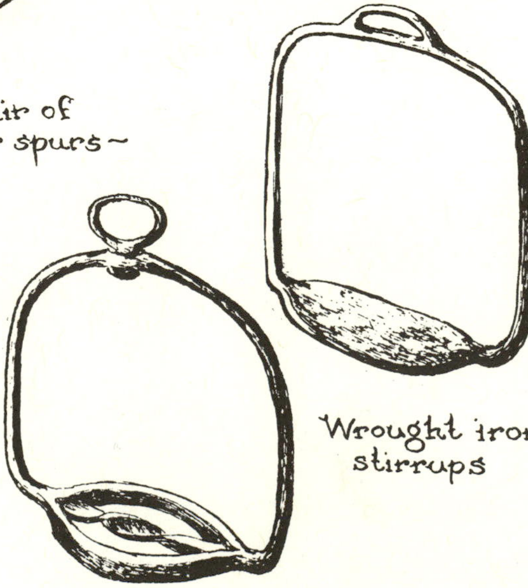

Wrought iron stirrups

Caltrops ~ scattered on the ground to slow cavalry

ARTILLERY

It was no small chore to move the cannon into action from the camp artillery park and down the rutted trails of the wilderness. To haul each 12-pounder (cannon were known by the weight of the ball they fired) with a bulk of 3200 pounds, all of 12 horses were required. Because the need for transport animals was great, dependable and sometimes undependable civilian owners were hired as drivers for the task. But if the Americans faced difficulties in moving their pieces, the British found it near impossible to place their greatly superior artillery in the right place at the right time.

Once on the battlefield, the cannon were maneuvered by their crews between regiments or battalions on the firing line. Occasionally they were placed in advance of the line or on a nearby hill. Solid shot was used at long range against the advancing British lines. When the enemy had advanced to 500 yards, grape shot or cannister sprayed the ranks. Exploding bombs from the howitzer and mortar also took their toll at this shorter range.

Artillery uniforms according to the 1779 order were blue coats faced and lined with scarlet with coat edging and button holes bound with narrow lace or tape.

AN ARTILLERYMAN'S INVENTORY LIST

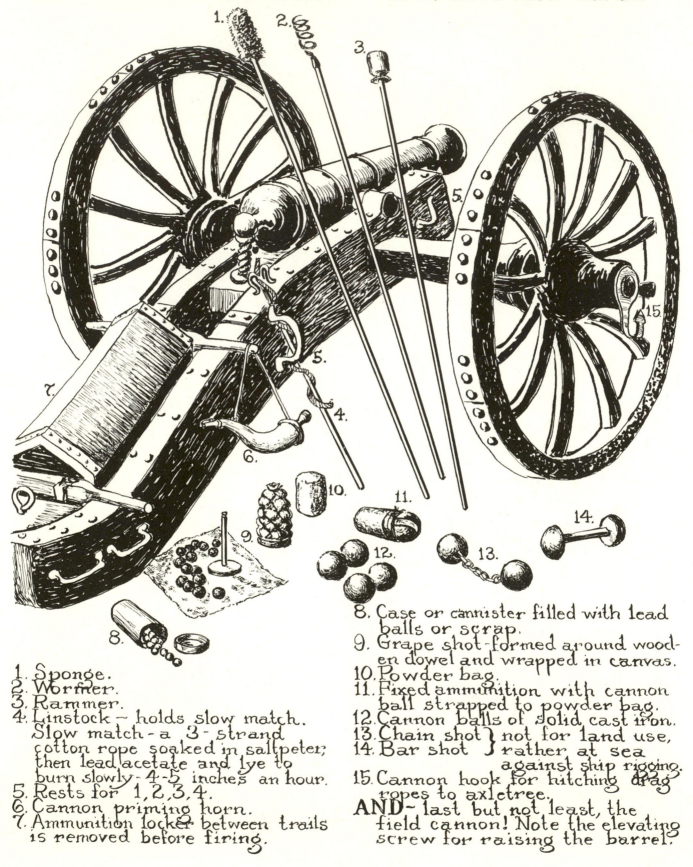

1. Sponge.
2. Wormer.
3. Rammer.
4. Linstock — holds slow match.
   Slow match - a 3-strand
   cotton rope soaked in saltpeter;
   then lead acetate and lye to
   burn slowly - 4-5 inches an hour.
5. Rests for 1, 2, 3, 4.
6. Cannon priming horn.
7. Ammunition locker between trails
   is removed before firing.

8. Case or cannister filled with lead
   balls or scrap.
9. Grape shot - formed around wood-
   en dowel and wrapped in canvas.
10. Powder bag.
11. Fixed ammunition with cannon
    ball strapped to powder bag.
12. Cannon balls of solid cast iron.
13. Chain shot } not for land use,
14. Bar shot } rather at sea
    against ship rigging.
15. Cannon hook for hitching drag
    ropes to axletree.
AND — last but not least, the
    field cannon! Note the elevating
    screw for raising the barrel.

LOADING AND FIRING THE CANNON

1. Cannon crew hauls the piece into firing position with drag ropes. Detachable handspike in rear gives more accurate placement.

2. Gunner's quadrant shows elevation by plumb line against scale arc. The elevating screw adjusts barrel to the proper angle.

3. Worm cleans bore of embers from previous firing.

4. Wet sheepskin sponge extinguishes sparks and cleans the bore.

5. Bag of powder is rammed down barrel.

6. Cannon ball or bag of grape shot is rammed to powder.

7. A brass pick is thrust down the vent to break open the powder bag.

8. Powder horn primes vent hole with powder.

9. Fire! Slow match on the linstock ignites priming.

THE ARTILLERY IN ACTION

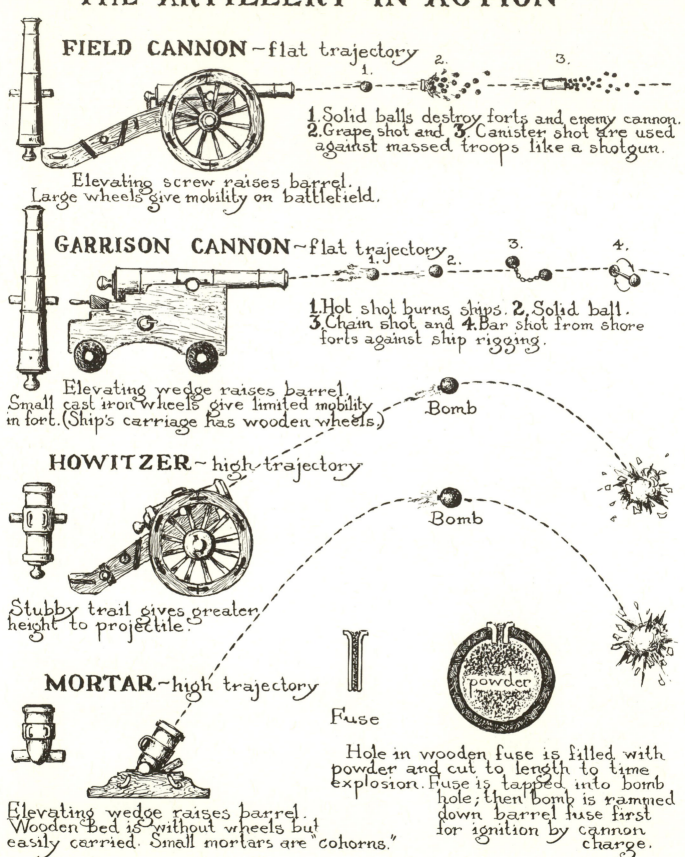

FIELD CANNON ~ flat trajectory

1. 2. 3.

1. Solid balls destroy forts and enemy cannon.
2. Grape shot and 3. Canister shot are used against massed troops like a shotgun.

Elevating screw raises barrel.
Large wheels give mobility on battlefield.

GARRISON CANNON ~ flat trajectory

1. 2. 3. 4.

1. Hot shot burns ships. 2. Solid ball.
3. Chain shot and 4. Bar shot from shore forts against ship rigging.

Elevating wedge raises barrel.
Small cast iron wheels give limited mobility in fort. (Ship's carriage has wooden wheels.)

HOWITZER ~ high trajectory

Bomb

Bomb

Stubby trail gives greater height to projectile.

MORTAR ~ high trajectory

Fuse

powder

Hole in wooden fuse is filled with powder and cut to length to time explosion. Fuse is tapped into bomb hole; then bomb is rammed down barrel fuse first for ignition by cannon charge.

Elevating wedge raises barrel.
Wooden bed is without wheels but easily carried. Small mortars are "cohorns."

46

DRUM COMMANDS

From the day that William Diamond's drum first rattled out "To Arms" for the Lexington militia, music played an important part in the Revolutionary Army. Each company, led by a fife and drum, stepped lively to such stirring tunes as "Yankee Doodle," "The White Cockade," "The Hessian," and "The Three Camps."

Commands in the Cavalry were blown on a bugle—but elsewhere in the army the fife and drums were the music makers. The drummer was considered the more important of the two, for he was the equivalent of the present-day bugler. By such descriptive rattles as the flam, ruff, paradiddle and ratamacue, the drum not only was used in marching but in giving commands. A call from the headquarter drummers would be repeated throughout the entire army in camp or on the march.

Steuben's regulations prescribed the following drum commands:

GENERAL - beat as a signal for the army to strike tents and prepare to march.

ASSEMBLY - repair to the colors.

MARCH - the troops move out.

REVEILLE - soldiers rise at daybreak and sentries to leave off challenging.

TATTOO - soldiers return to tents to remain until reveille beating next morning.

TO ARMS - alarm to take up weapons.

PARLEY - beat when a conference with the enemy is desired.

47

FIFE AND DRUM

The fife, drawn half-scale, is iron and was found where the Northern Department had its headquarters in August, 1777. Saratoga National Park, N.Y.

The playing of taps was unknown in the Continental Army.

The drum cases were wooden, strung with ropes on the sides and snares of heavy gut across the bottom head for greater resonance. The heavy sticks could rattle out commands well above the din of musketry.

Fifes were simply turned wooden, occasionally iron, hollow tubes with a blow hole and six finger holes. Although these rather crude and often off-pitched instruments could not match the quality French horns, clarinets and bassoons of the British bands, the enthusiastic American fifers whistled up many a merry tune for the troops.

In the latter years of the war, the coats of the drummers and fifers had reversed colors. For example, New England musicians wore white coats with blue facings. In the confusion of battle, these contrasting uniforms could be easily spotted to issue maneuver orders.

48

MARKS OF AN OFFICER

GORGET ~ a remnant of the armored knight's throat protection, the gilt or silver crescent was hung from the neck by a ribbon. Engraved designs varied from the familiar "Don't Tread On Me" coiled rattlesnake design to a trophy of flags and arms.

But the gorget was never officially adopted by the Continental Army, as it was in the English, Hessian and French forces. Although worn occasionally by officers in the field early in the war, the practice gradually fell out of favor.

EPAULETTE ~ this descendant of the shoulder strap was of gold or silver lace, and indicated the officer's rank.

SASH ~ a long length of red cloth, often of silk, and was wrapped around the waist.

SWORD ~ carried by a black or white shoulder or waist belt.

SPONTOON ~ a pole arm carried by all officers on foot duty. Many were the shapes of the spear head. In 1778, the spontoon was standardized to a staff six feet long and one and one-quarter inches in diameter. The iron part was to be one foot long.

Spontoons were preferred to muskets, for there was no loading and firing to detract attention from the troops.

EPAULETTES AND LEADERSHIP

COMMISSIONED OFFICERS

Major General - Two epaulettes, each with two stars.

Brigadier General - Two epaulettes, each with one star.

Colonel - Two epaulettes plain.

Lieutenant Colonel - The same.

Major - The same.

Captain - One epaulette on the right shoulder.

Subaltern (Lieutenant and Ensign) - One epaulette on the left shoulder.

NON-COMMISSIONED OFFICERS

Sergeant - epaulette on right shoulder, red.

Corporal - epaulette on left shoulder, green.

Officers'-of gold or silver lace & wire.

LEADERSHIP

The men who wore the epaulettes entered the army with many preconceived attitudes. Some inherited the British officers' aloofness to the rank and file. Some southern officers, used to managing large plantations with servants and slaves, were overbearing with their authority. Again, some officers from the north, raised in the democratic ideal of equality, found it difficult to make their neighbors obey their commands. Soldiers disliked the idea of saluting boyhood friends from nearby farms.

However, Washington sliced through these old attitudes by insisting on strong discipline from an officer whom the men could respect. Unquestioning obedience to orders in camp could mean victory in the field.

Von Steuben agreed wholeheartedly with strict discipline. He also emphasized in his "Regulations for the Order and Discipline of the Troops of the United States" that a firm hand must be tempered with understanding and concern. He wrote that "His [the officer's] first object should be to gain the love of his men by treating them with every possible kindness and humanity, inquiring into their complaints, and when well founded, seeing them redressed"

SWORDS

HUNTING SWORD - long - more efficient combat. Carried likely to see interesting animal or bird heads. The chain prevented the sword from slipping from the protected from slipping blade.

less than two feet on the hunt than by officers not battle. Have pommels, often bird heads prevented from slipping hand, and the hand blows or to the blade.

SMALL SWORD - most widely used by officers. Because of finely wrought brass or silver mountings, it was a favorite as a dress sword.
The two rings, "pas-d'ânes," set above the protective counterguard, were remnants of Spanish fencing styles of the 1600's, when fingers were hooked through the holes.

SABER - carried by many foot officers and all cavalrymen. Pommels ranged from simple balls and urns to lion and dog heads. The lion head, pride of His Majesty's army, was decidedly unpopular after 1775 in America!
The guard was of brass, with pierced designs.
It was a sturdy, efficient weapon.

BELTS AND SCABBARDS
Sword belts were either black or white, and worn from the shoulder or about the waist by officers and the cavalry.

The **SHOULDER BELT** carried the scabbard by means of a frog. This loop of leather bore a slit through which was inserted the scabbard prong. This style belt was preferred by the cavalry.

WAIST BELT with a hook or hanger. The metal hook carried the scabbard by means of two attached chains.

WAIST BELT with a frog.

WAIST BELT with two leather straps and snaps to hold the rings of the scabbard.

POLE ARMS

Pole arms were edged weapons with a handle longer than the blade. In America, variations were as many as the imaginative blacksmiths who made them.

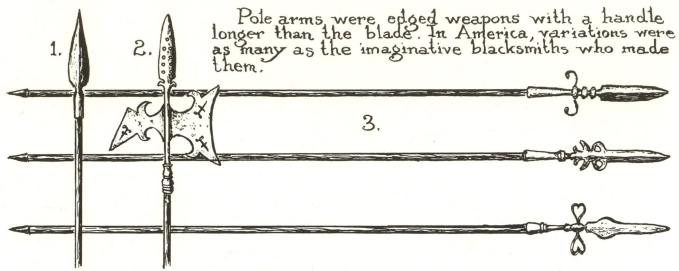

1. 2. 3.

1. TRENCH PIKES — double-edged iron spears were used in large numbers to defend or attack fortifications.

Lacking a bayonet, the rifleman also found the pike useful in outreaching a bayoneted musket and as a rest for steady aiming.

Around the camp, pikes were put to use as tent poles.

2. HALBERD — double-edged spear with elongated shaft was slotted for a thin sheet of iron, shaped with a blade and beak. It was not a combat weapon, but rather served as a badge of authority for sergeants and often corporals. It also made an excellent target for sharpshooters and so was replaced by light muskets (fusils) and bayonets early in the Revolution.

3. SPONTOON — was a rugged double-edged spear with an enlarged base, often having a cross bar below it. It was carried by officers as a symbol of authority AND a combat weapon as well. It was not replaced by the fusil and bayonet, for it was felt that no officer could command his troops properly while loading his flintlock.

Punishment "by the halberds" consisted of lashing two halberds into an "X", then spread-eagling the offender on it with ankles and wrists tied securely. In this awkward position, he was the butt of much ridicule around the camp.

The spontoon served as an "at home" sign for the officer when stuck in the ground in front of his tent. At night, it served as a convenient lantern post.

SALUTE THAT OFFICER!

The soldier under arms saluted an officer by halting and facing him, then bringing his musket to "shoulder firelock".

Officer

To "shoulder firelock", the butt was held in the left hand, the arm held naturally at the side, and the stock against the left shoulder perpendicular to the body.

The officer under arms returned the salute by bringing his fusil to "order firelock" (butt on the ground and against the right side of the body). The hat was then removed with the left hand and brought away from the left side with a sweeping motion, crown toward the body.

The soldier not under arms and wearing a tricorn hat, saluted by halting and facing the officer. He then removed his hat in a sweeping motion to the right side, crown toward the body. The right foot was brought slightly back.

A soldier wearing a cap, as shown on the light infantry man on the right, did not remove his cover to salute. The more elaborate headgear would make this difficult. Instead, he brought his hand to the cap and held it in this position until the officer had continued on his way.

The officer returned the salute in the same way as the soldier at left.

PISTOLS

Officers, cavalry, sailors, and selected infantrymen such as Glover's versatile Marblehead Regiment carried pistols.

The large cavalry "horse" pistols were held securely on horseback in leather holsters. Officers and infantrymen carried the pistol in their belts, while the sailors used the belt hook on the reverse side of their pistols to attach to the belt.

BRITISH CAVALRY "HORSE" PISTOLS

Old Model   New 1780 Model

Most widely carried by the Americans

FRENCH CAVALRY

HOLSTER - The heavy black leather flared at the top to receive both the butt and the projecting cock.

Model 1763
Iron furniture

Model 1776
Iron furniture

AMERICAN PISTOLS

Officer's Pistol

Officers purchased their own side arms and because most were made in England before the war they resembled the British service pistols. They were shorter, lighter, and often with silver mountings.

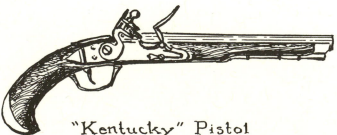

"Kentucky" Pistol

In many ways this distinctly American pistol was like its big brother, the "Kentucky" rifle. The sights and lock were smaller versions, both had similar brass ramrod pipes, and the pistol was frequently rifled. It was a valued side arm for American officers.

KNAPSACKS AND HAVERSACKS

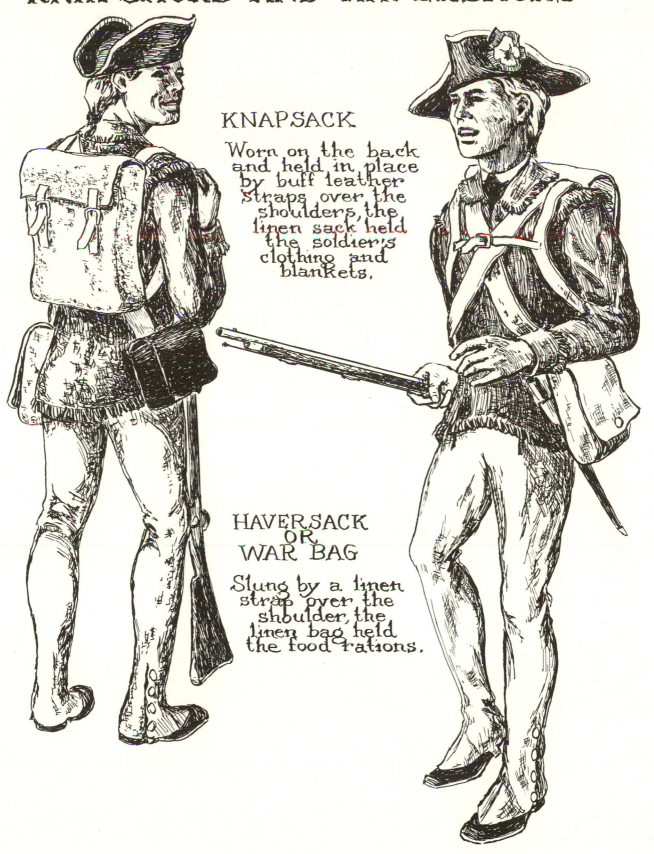

KNAPSACK

Worn on the back and held in place by buff leather straps over the shoulders, the linen sack held the soldier's clothing and blankets.

HAVERSACK OR WAR BAG

Slung by a linen strap over the shoulder, the linen bag held the food rations.

CANTEENS

Wooden canteen with interlocking wooden straps.

Wooden canteen with iron straps and wire belt holders.

Water not only expanded the wooden joints for a tight fit but also cooled the contents by outside evaporation.

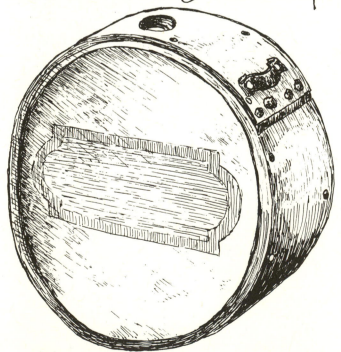

Wooden canteen with bent wood strip pegged to sides. The nailed leather strips hold the belt.

Tin canteen

MORE CANTEENS

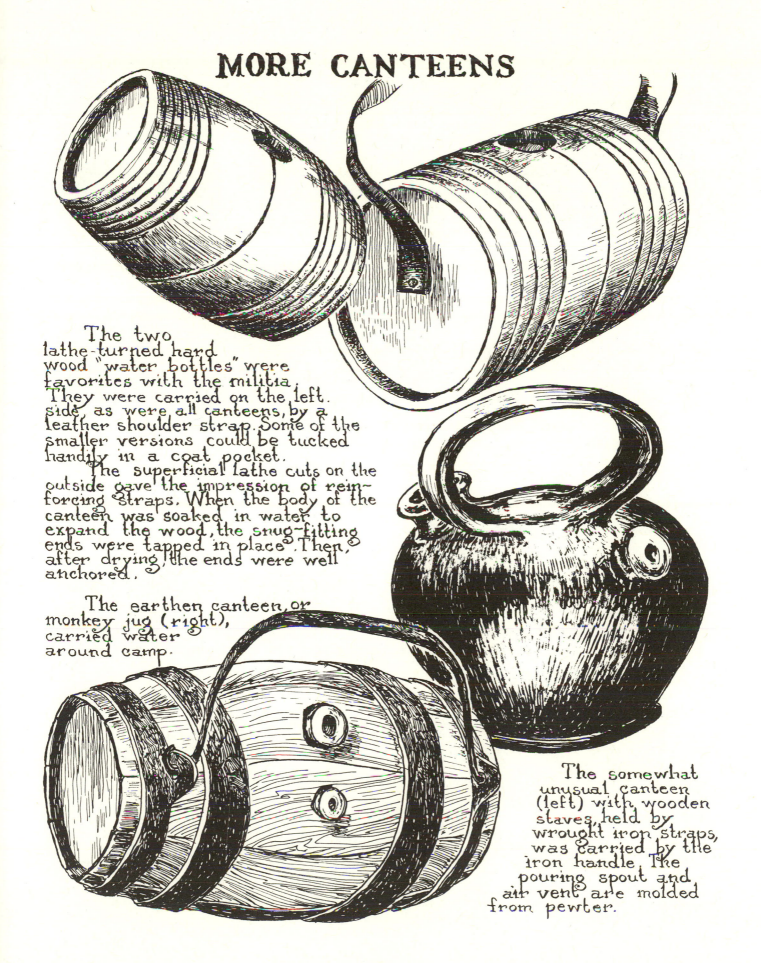

The two lathe-turned hard wood "water bottles" were favorites with the militia. They were carried on the left side, as were all canteens, by a leather shoulder strap. Some of the smaller versions could be tucked handily in a coat pocket.

The superficial lathe cuts on the outside gave the impression of reinforcing straps. When the body of the canteen was soaked in water to expand the wood, the snug-fitting ends were tapped in place. Then, after drying, the ends were well anchored.

The earthen canteen, or monkey jug (right), carried water around camp.

The somewhat unusual canteen (left) with wooden staves, held by wrought iron straps, was carried by the iron handle. The pouring spout and air vent are molded from pewter.

STARTING THE FIRE

A small tin box easily carried the fixings for a fire - the flint or a piece of clear quartz, a strip of charred cloth, and tinder from shredded cedar bark.

Steel for striking the flint came from the back side of a jack knife blade or a wrought steel striker. An old file also sparked well.

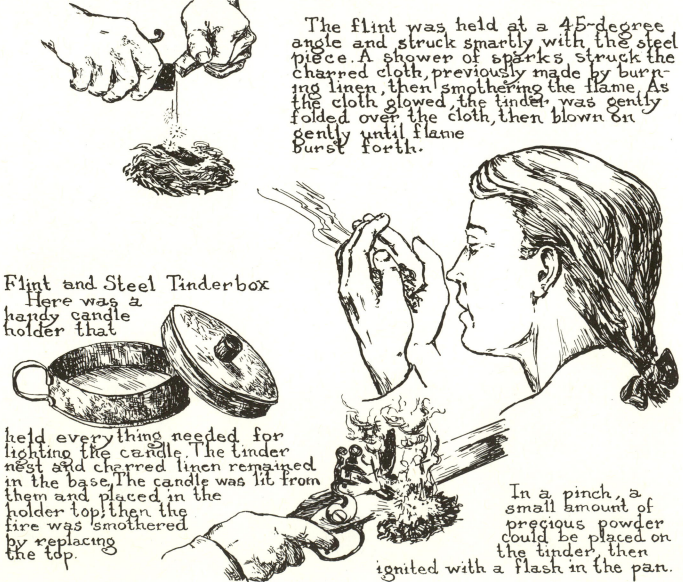

The flint was held at a 45-degree angle and struck smartly with the steel piece. A shower of sparks struck the charred cloth, previously made by burning linen, then smothering the flame. As the cloth glowed, the tinder was gently folded over the cloth, then blown on gently until flame burst forth.

Flint and Steel Tinderbox
Here was a handy candle holder that held everything needed for lighting the candle. The tinder nest and charred linen remained in the base. The candle was lit from them and placed in the holder top, then the fire was smothered by replacing the top.

In a pinch, a small amount of precious powder could be placed on the tinder, then ignited with a flash in the pan.

LIGHTING

CANDLEWOOD

was as near as the handiest pitch pine tree. Once sawed into blocks, splinters about the size of a large tallow candle could be split off. When several were thrust between stones of the fireplace or into the hearth, the brightly burning sticks gave off a tolerable amount of light, for reading. Although the smoke was considerable, most disappeared up the chimney flu.

HISTORIC LANTERN

The top lantern was one of the two that hung from the Old North Church. Should Paul Revere be captured trying to leave Boston to warn the countryside, patriots across the Charles River would still be alerted by the lanterns. Two lights meant that the British would go by "sea" or across the river to march on the munitions stored at Concord.

The lower lantern is often wrongly called "the Revere lantern," and was actually made between 1820~1850. It is difficult to imagine the pinpoints of light from a pierced tin being seen clear across the river!

SOLDIERS' CANDLE HOLDERS

Easily carried, these were favorites with the Continentals.

Brass

Wrought iron

COOKING ON THE MARCH

Units of six soldiers were mess mates as well as tent mates. Each mess was issued a cast iron kettle, heavy enough to make hand carrying difficult during the march. Perhaps the army's route could best be followed by the discarded pots that dotted the roadside. The six men also were given a tomahawk and the rations for the day.

When the army was on the move, each soldier received daily a skimpy and unappetizing pound of beef and flour. As for the meat, it was generally broiled on a stick over the open fire. Cooking utensils were just another scarcity.

But the greatest gastronomic distress to be found in the temporary camp was the fire cake. The recipe was simple. Flour was placed on a flat rock and cold water added. The mixture was pommelled into a paste, then daubed on another flat stone and set upright near the fire. The fire cake was thereby charred on the outside, leaving raw dough inside. Here was a dish that only the stoutest or hungriest Continental could relish.

Note the old bayonet, bent to form a pot hook, and the bar shot, used as a makeshift andiron.

CAMP RATIONS & OFFICERS' COOKWARE

Army rations were reasonably mouth-watering when the Continentals were fortunate enough to camp by a city. There were well-supplied niceties such as corned beef, pork, fresh beef and fish daily as well as rice, Indian meal, hog's lard, potatoes, peas, beans, onions, turnips, fresh bread and hard bread.

But in the usual back hills encampments, a menu such as this was a vague memory. Then lean rations of salt pork and beef were as tasty as burned gun powder. Generally the soldier preferred this poor offering to be fried and well done, rather than broiled as suggested by the officers.

There were so few fresh vegetables available that salads were made from greens around camp such as watercress and lamb's quarter. Soups helped disguise the fare, but generally were disliked by the American troops.

One permanent camp luxury was fresh-baked bread. From these brick and occasionally iron monsters erupted great quantities of crisp loaves. Here was a welcome change from the soggy fire cakes in the temporary encampments!

Camp stove of iron. Broiler was hinged and upper feet support frying pan.

Brass tent cooking pot with iron legs and handle.

Copper camp kettle with iron legs and wood handle.

FORKS, PLATES, AND INGENUITY

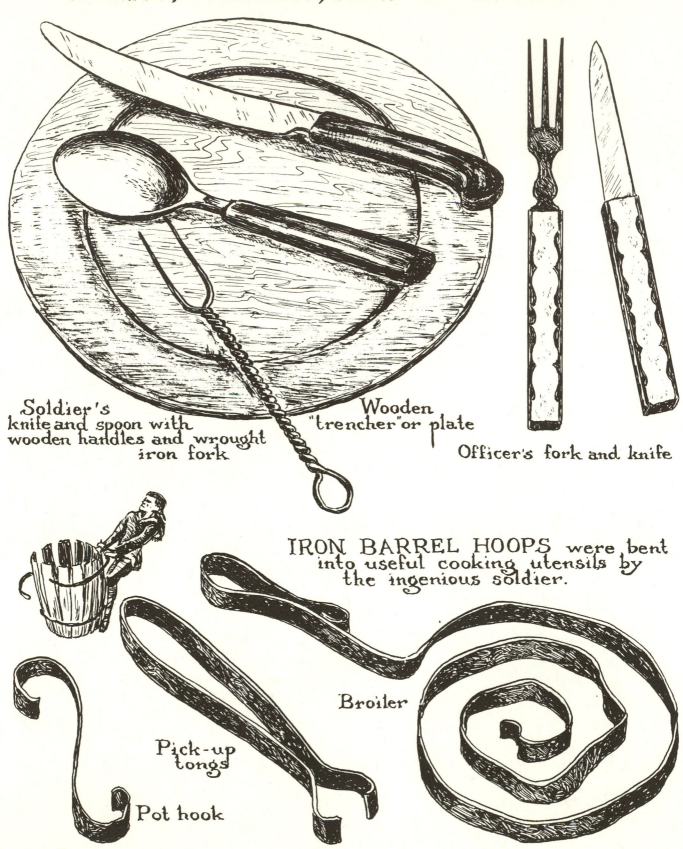

Soldier's knife and spoon with wooden handles and wrought iron fork

Wooden "trencher" or plate

Officer's fork and knife

IRON BARREL HOOPS were bent into useful cooking utensils by the ingenious soldier.

Broiler

Pick-up tongs

Pot hook

THAT'S THE SPIRIT!

Realizing that good soldiering could only be diluted by alcohol, Washington took a firm stand early in the war. All taverns were placed out of bounds to the troops, and any soldier disobeying this order was roundly punished. Any shop keeper guilty of such sales was routed out and his building used to quarter troops.

The thirsty soldier could, however, "raise his spirits" at the sutler's tent. In each brigade, this civilian store keeper was authorized to sell his wares to the military. Among his liquid refreshments were home made spirits, gin, rum, cordials, strong beer, common beer, and "cyder-royal." Thirsty or not, the soldier could purchase no more than half a pint of spirits per day.

Washington's firm hand relaxed but slightly when it came to the issuing of liquor from the army stores. Details returned from such fatiguing duty as long marches, guard duty, or heavy labor were given rations enough to warm their innards.

The squatty, bulbous based bottles of the previous century were replaced by those typically found in the Revolutionary camps. They were free-blown with a cylindrical body and a straight tapered neck with a ring of glass near the top. The indented bottom retained its pontil, or broken connection with the blow pipe. They were usually olive amber or green.

An occasional bottle could be found that was blown into a mold as drawn in 3. There were also flat-sided specimens called case bottles as in 4 & 5. Officers carried these remedies for cold camp nights in boxes of twelve.

BATTALION LOG HOUSE CITY

Companies or "platoons" of infantry were composed of twenty-five to fifty men. A standard number of companies formed a battalion of about two hundred soldiers (as sketched). Two battalions were combined into a regiment, the basic infantry unit of the Continental Army. A brigade was made up of two or more regiments.

The following buildings were to be found on a well-drained hillside:

A. Hospitals — small units separated from camp.
B. Artillery Park — all ammunition issued here.
C. Supply Trains — food rations issued here every few days.
D. Kitchens — ovens for baking bread.
E. Officers' Cabins — large, less crowded and varied construction.
F. Soldiers' Huts — identically built in two or more rows and divided by camp roads of varying widths.
G. Color Line — Regimental flags planted here, as well as stacked muskets in good weather. When the "Alarm" was beaten, the army formed on this line, ready for action.
H. Parade Ground

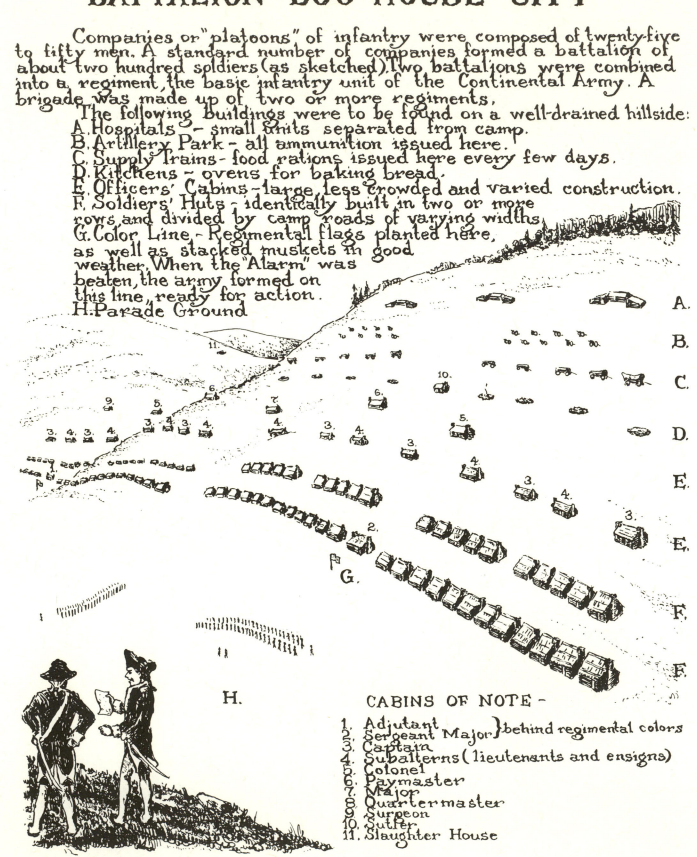

CABINS OF NOTE —

1. Adjutant }behind regimental colors
2. Sergeant Major
3. Captain
4. Subalterns (lieutenants and ensigns)
5. Colonel
6. Paymaster
7. Major
8. Quartermaster
9. Surgeon
10. Sutler
11. Slaughter House

64

THE FELLING AX BUILDS THE SOLDIERS' HUT

Oak, walnut and chestnut were favored woods for construction.

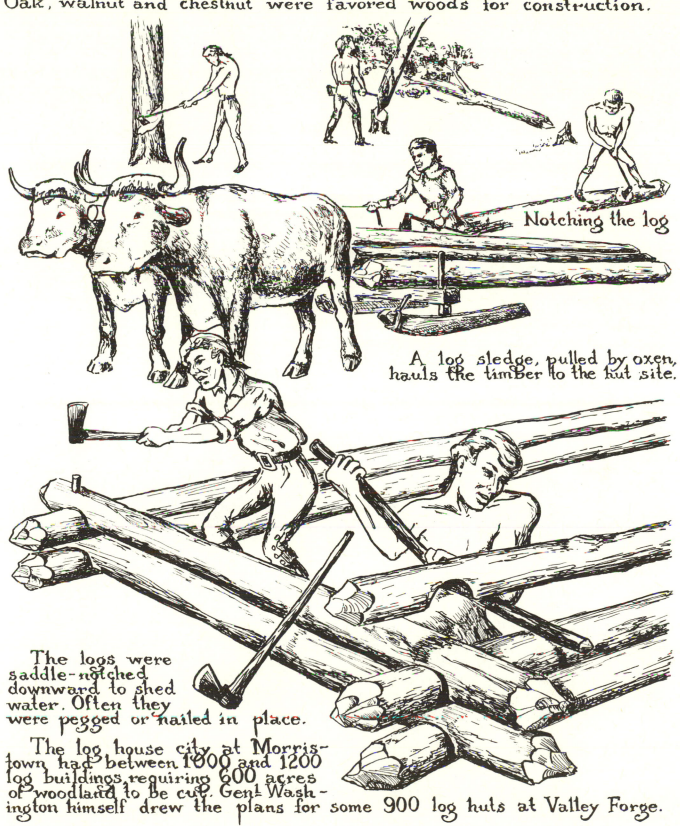

Notching the log

A log sledge, pulled by oxen, hauls the timber to the hut site.

The logs were saddle-notched downward to shed water. Often they were pegged or nailed in place.

The log house city at Morristown had between 1000 and 1200 log buildings, requiring 600 acres of woodland to be cut. Genl Washington himself drew the plans for some 900 log huts at Valley Forge.

HUT CONSTRUCTION

The hut building continued according to a uniform plan. Each must be 14 feet long and 16 feet wide. When the height of 6½ feet was reached, logs from both sides were extended 1 foot front and back. On these rested the notched eave logs. More parallel roof logs were added as the side logs gradually angled up to the peak.

Although some roofs were covered with boards or slabs, while others were thatched with straw, frequently crude shingles were cut. This added nicety required more than the all-purpose felling axe.

First, thick trees were sawed in lengths of 4 feet. These were squared, then shingles split off the block with a long-bladed wedge or froe. This tool was struck with a club-like maul as the froe twisted the length of board free.

Two layers of shingles were laid in each row to cover the under joints,

These were joined to the eave and roof beams.

Chocking between the logs with clay or mud.

The single chimney was notched into the center of a side. The inside stone lining was laid to the level of the eaves. At times, the logs were begun on the stone base instead of encasing it.

OFFICERS' AND SOLDIERS' HUTS

Officers' hut
(left)

Soldiers' hut
(below)

Officer huts were of individual design and construction, and boasted of two or more doors and windows. Two fire places and chimneys were at either end of the hut. Larger in size than that of the soldiers', there were no more than two to four officers in each of the buildings.

Soldiers' huts ~ Groups of six men formed a "mess" to cook and eat together. Two such groups also bunked together. After these twelve built their huts according to specifications, wooden bunks were made. These were elevated off the dirt floor to protect against the cold and dampness. Wooden racks, known as "horses", were also made for arms and equipment.

Ventilation was a problem in these crowded one-room huts. At least two windows were required, although they were rarely cut until spring. Better circulation was possible when the soldiers plastered less mud be-tween the logs. Air was purified by the foul-smelling smoke of burning gunpowder. The odor of tar was also, unfortunately, considered beneficial.

TENTS

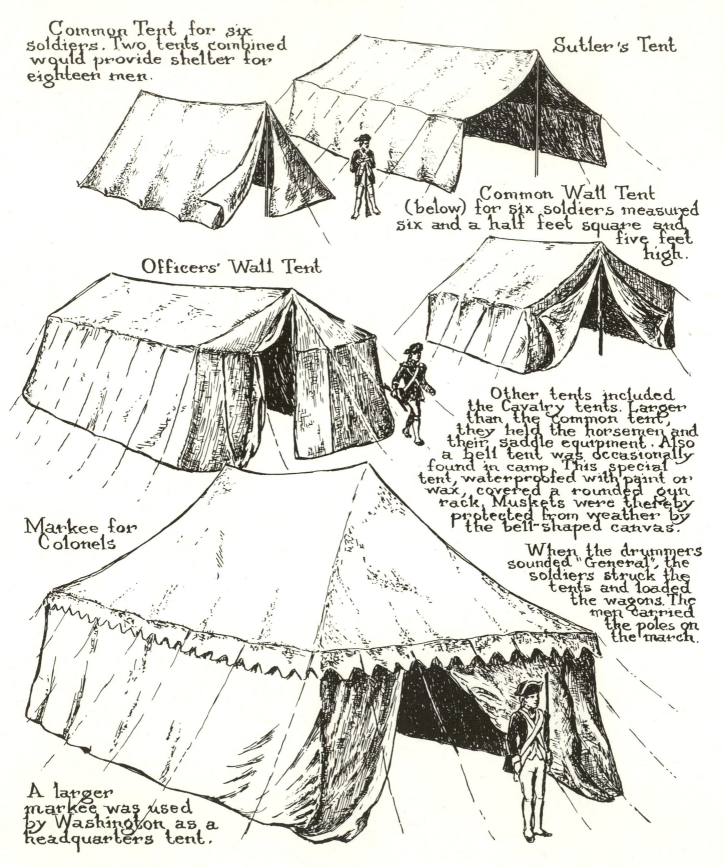

Common Tent for six soldiers. Two tents combined would provide shelter for eighteen men.

Sutler's Tent

Common Wall Tent (below) for six soldiers measured six and a half feet square and five feet high.

Officers' Wall Tent

Other tents included the Cavalry tents. Larger than the common tent, they held the horsemen and their saddle equipment. Also a bell tent was occasionally found in camp. This special tent, waterproofed with paint or wax, covered a rounded gun rack. Muskets were thereby protected from weather by the bell-shaped canvas.

When the drummers sounded "General", the soldiers struck the tents and loaded the wagons. The men carried the poles on the march.

Markee for Colonels

A larger markee was used by Washington as a headquarters tent.

CAMP SLAUGHTER HOUSE

Because of the distinctive odors and difficulties with cleanliness, the slaughter house was located a safe mile from the camp. It was also the last mile for the livestock that met their fate there. Nothing went to waste. After all that was edible was removed, the salvage operation extended to all that was not.

FROM FAT TO SOAP

The women attached to each company were issued a cask for lye-making. This barrel was filled with layers of straw and wood ashes; then boiling water was poured over the contents. The amber-colored lye dripped

from a hole in the bottom of the cask and into a pail, ready for the next step.

The ration of fat from the slaughter house was placed in a large camp kettle, the lye added and the mixture brought to a brisk boil. After several hours of back-breaking stirring, the jelled soap was ready for cutting into cakes for the soldiers.

FROM HOOVES TO OIL

Neat's foot oil was made in camp by boiling animal hooves. This valuable oil was the only means of protecting metal from rusting. Barrels and locks in contact with burned powder were especially apt to rust.

FROM HIDES TO LEATHER

Although sheep and calf skins were prepared for drum heads or sacks for cannisters, tanning of the leather was difficult and time-consuming in camp. It was best left for civilian tanners. Therefore the larger cattle and oxen hides were sold or exchanged for shoes. Two hides were also carried with every piece of artillery, to be wet and wrapped around the barrel when hot from firing, thereby "refreshing" the piece.

FROM HORNS TO POWDER HORNS

The smooth and nicely curved oxen horns, free from twists or rings, were highly prized for powder containers.

BIRTH OF THE BREASTWORK

FASCINES (pronounced fasheens) were bundles of sticks, bound firmly together in lengths of five to twelve feet, and trimmed square at the ends.

BILL HOOK
This was just the tool for clearing a new camp-site of brush. Once done, these same sticks could be put to good use in building entrenchments to protect the camp. Fascines and gabions were readied prior to the actual digging, for they formed the frame of the breastwork.

GABIONS
(pronounced gab-beens) were cylinders of woven brush. A skeleton of sticks was driven into the ground to form a circle two or more feet in diameter.

The fresh-cut, pliable brush was then interwoven around the stakes to form a bottomless basket.

BREASTWORK COMPLETED

The back-breaking job of entrenching began by staking the outline on the ground. Generally this was angular to allow for cross fire. The first line of gabion baskets was placed on this outline; then a depth of two or more additional rows were staggered to close the joints. Next, the trench was dug behind the first row, and the dirt thrown into the gabions.

Once the gabions were filled and covered with dirt, the bundles of stakes, or fascines, were laid on the inside and outside of the dirt face, anchored with four-foot-long stakes, then covered with earth and sod.

WAGONS

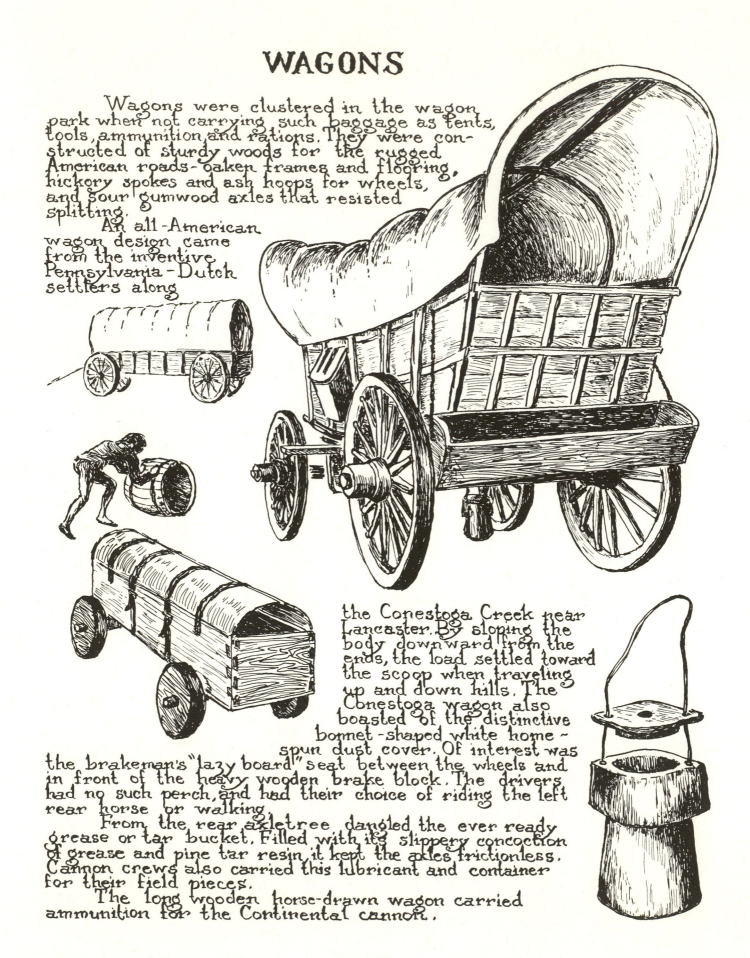

Wagons were clustered in the wagon park when not carrying such baggage as tents, tools, ammunition, and rations. They were constructed of sturdy woods for the rugged American roads—oaken frames and flooring, hickory spokes and ash hoops for wheels, and sour gumwood axles that resisted splitting.

An all-American wagon design came from the inventive Pennsylvania-Dutch settlers along the Conestoga Creek near Lancaster. By sloping the body downward from the ends, the load settled toward the scoop when traveling up and down hills. The Conestoga wagon also boasted of the distinctive bonnet-shaped white home-spun dust cover. Of interest was the brakeman's "lazy board" seat between the wheels and in front of the heavy wooden brake block. The drivers had no such perch, and had their choice of riding the left rear horse or walking.

From the rear axletree dangled the ever ready grease or tar bucket. Filled with its slippery concoction of grease and pine tar resin it kept the axles frictionless. Cannon crews also carried this lubricant and container for their field pieces.

The long wooden horse-drawn wagon carried ammunition for the Continental cannon.

72

DISEASE IN CAMP

The isolated towns in America effectively prevented illnesses from spreading. But when soldiers from all the thirteen states met in camp, disease went on the rampage. Many under the age of twenty were fair game for these germs, while those over thirty withstood them better with whatever immunity they had acquired from previous contacts.

Of little consolation to the stricken soldier was the fact that the physicians' knowledge of his disease was meager. Bacteria and viruses were unknown. The formation of pus in a wound could be expected, for sterilization techniques were primitive indeed. And because the causes of most diseases were uncertain, the method of spread was prevented with difficulty. There were no diagnostic aids as stethoscopes and thermometers. Little was known of man's inner workings, and diagnoses were generally made by simply observing the patient.

CAMP HOSPITALS

B = BUNKS - feet toward the fire

F = OPEN FIRE PLACES

Congress called for a hospital plan for a twenty thousand soldier army. Caring for this optimistic number were a director general and chief physician (paid at four dollars daily), four surgeons, one apothecary, twenty surgeon's mates, two store keepers, and one nurse for every ten patients. Women in camp acted as nurses and received the regular pay.

A more realistic hospital change was soon made, however. One surgeon and five mates were provided for every thousand men.

Early in the war, hospitals became a catch-all for disease. Desperately ill men were stuffed into small rooms, frequently lying heel to head. They shared their germs with damp and dirty clothing, and waited out their misery on unchanged straw. Fortunate was the soldier who could leave the hospital alive and free of some new malady.

By 1777, the large, overcrowded general hospital was replaced by the smaller buildings drawn here. The loosely chocked log hospitals gave free circulation of air and the series of isolated units prevented man-to-man infection. The soldiers appreciated this, and cheerfully accepted their cold room and the dirt floor. The typhus-carrying lice could no longer spread the dread jail fever.

Cleanliness became important and sacks were filled with fresh straw. When a man died or was discharged, the bedding was washed and aired and the straw burned. Diarrhea caused by typhoid-contaminating bedding and clothes was less frequent.

Recovery from fevers was facilitated and dysenteries were minimized when the patients were moved away from the cold walls. Less crowding meant fewer coughs and sneezes to spread "pleurisy" (pneumonia).

Each of the small hospitals contained open fires without chimneys. Smoke escaped through a hole in the ridge of the roof. It was thought that the free smoke in the room could purify the "putrid" air. Twice a week sulfur, pitch, tar or gunpowder were burned in the hope of ridding the air of germs.

DOCTORS AND DISEASE

Disease in camp proved far more formidable than the Redcoats on the battlefield. In 1776, for example, one thousand Americans were killed by musketry or bayonet, and another twelve hundred received battlefield wounds. Six thousand more were interned in prison camps, while a staggering ten thousand lost their lives to illness.

Forming the defence line against the pestilence were twelve hundred physicians that served varying stints in the war years. They represented about a third of the practicing doctors in the colonies. Of this total of thirty-five hundred professional men, only two hundred had received medical degrees from the two schools in Philadelphia and New York. The vast number of physicians, therefore, had to gain their knowledge through a three- to seven-year apprenticeship.

The diseases that confronted these determined men of varied training were formidable. Then unknown were the microscopic bacteria, the smaller rickettsia, and the still smaller viral infections. Yet they did what they could, and some of the prophylaxis and treatments were admirable for those difficult times.

JAIL FEVER, HOSPITAL FEVER, OR PUTRID FEVER ~
Typhoid – progressive fever, rose-colored spots on chest and abdomen, delirium and coma (bacteria spread by excrement on food, clothing, bedding and by flies)
Typhus - similar signs, but with a generalized petechial or hemorrhagic rash (rickettsia spread by the bite of the body louse)

Body Louse

enlarged

DYSENTERY OR DIARRHEA ~
fever, abdominal cramps, frequent stools of blood, pus and mucus (bacteria spread by contaminated food, water and flies)

WHITE PLAGUE ~ fever, cough - often with blood, chest pain and weight loss. (tuberculosis bacteria infected lung and other parts of the body, spread by coughing or eating contaminated food or water)

PLEURISY ~ fever, sharp pain and "stitches" in the chest, cough (bacterial pneumonia because of lowered resistance)

SMALLPOX ~ skin eruptions resulting in pits and scars, headache and muscle pains (virus spread from rash, coughing, sneezing or on clothing)

AGUE ~ chills, intermittently spiking fever, finally ending with profuse sweating (malaria parasites spread by mosquito bite, then entering the soldier's red blood cells)

SCURVY ~ bleeding into skin and mouth, swelling of legs, low blood count (lack of vitamin C from diet deficient in fresh fruits and vegetables)

℞ TREATMENT ~ Jail fever, dysentery, white plague, pleurisy and smallpox were better prevented than treated by well-cooked food, pure water from the middle of the stream, burning hospital straw after an illness, washing and airing of bedding. Specific treatments included isolation without crowding and good food. Specific for ague was "the bark" of the Cinchona tree (quinine). Scurvy responded promptly to fresh greens and ripe fruit.

REMEDIES

From the camp medical chest came roots and herbs, long on Latin names and short on curing. But the unfortunate soldier could count on one or all of the following "cure-alls" to be inflicted, thereby increasing his sorry lot considerably.

CATHARTICS OR LAXATIVES (calomel, jalap, nitre, Peruvian bark, and snake root) for purging out sickness.

EMETICS (tartar emetic, warm water and honey) for vomiting out the illness by a different pathway.

ENEMAS - still another method of flushing out illness.

BLISTERING - a caustic solution was applied to the skin to raise blisters. It was thought that the irritation drew the inflammation outside, but it succeeded only in changing the character of the soldier's pain.

BLOODLETTING - to rid the body of disease poisons, "bad" blood was drawn out by cutting an arm vein. An average of one pint was drawn, but the more serious the illness, the more was let. The badly weakened patient was supposed to regenerate his loss in several hours from some mysterious body gland. Actually, several weeks were required for the bone marrow to replace the weakened soldier's loss.

The favored spring lancet cut open a blood vessel when the cocked blade was freed by the side lever.

Thomas Jefferson's lancet, Monticello, Virginia

Although the fleam was a veterinary instrument used for bloodletting, its many blades may have been used to bleed both man and beast. Regimental physicians did the best they could with the few instruments on hand.

A POX ON YOU!

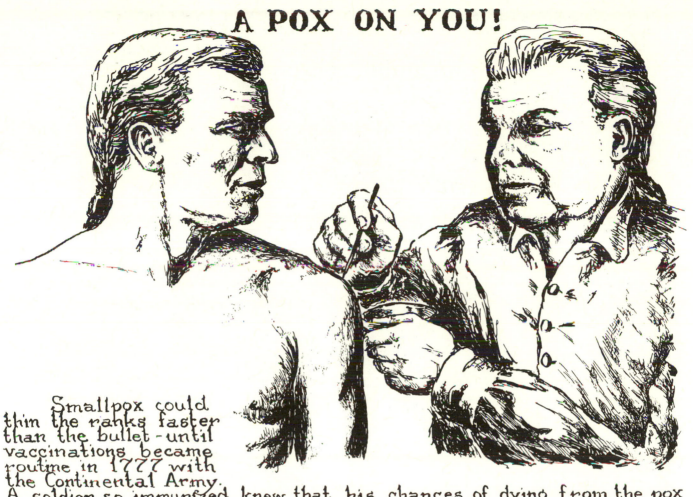

Smallpox could thin the ranks faster than the bullet - until vaccinations became routine in 1777 with the Continental Army. A soldier so immunized knew that his chances of dying from the pox were small - but one in four hundred. Prior to this, sixty out of four hundred would surely lose their lives when this dread disease struck camp. The saying "A pox on you!" no longer held the meaning that it did in pre-Revolutionary days.

The technique was simple. Young, healthy soldiers, who had contracted a mild case of smallpox, were chosen as donors. On the twelfth or thirteenth day, when the scabs had dried and become less potent, the crusts were removed. The physician then transferred these offerings to the left arm of the uninfected soldiery. This was done by a small puncture or a long incision from a needle or a lancet. To prevent the vaccine from flowing away or being diluted, no more than a single drop of blood was drawn. No plaster or bandage was placed on the puncture site, for the vaccine might spread under the covering and produce a massive pox.

After the procedure, the inevitable laxative was given, and twelve to fourteen ounces of blood let to regulate the eruptive fever after inoculation. As if to make amends, the patient was kept clean, isolated, and given fresh food. It was logical, therefore, that the vaccinations be given in the summer when supplies were available and resistance high.

folding lancet with bone handles

77

MEDICAL INSTRUMENTS

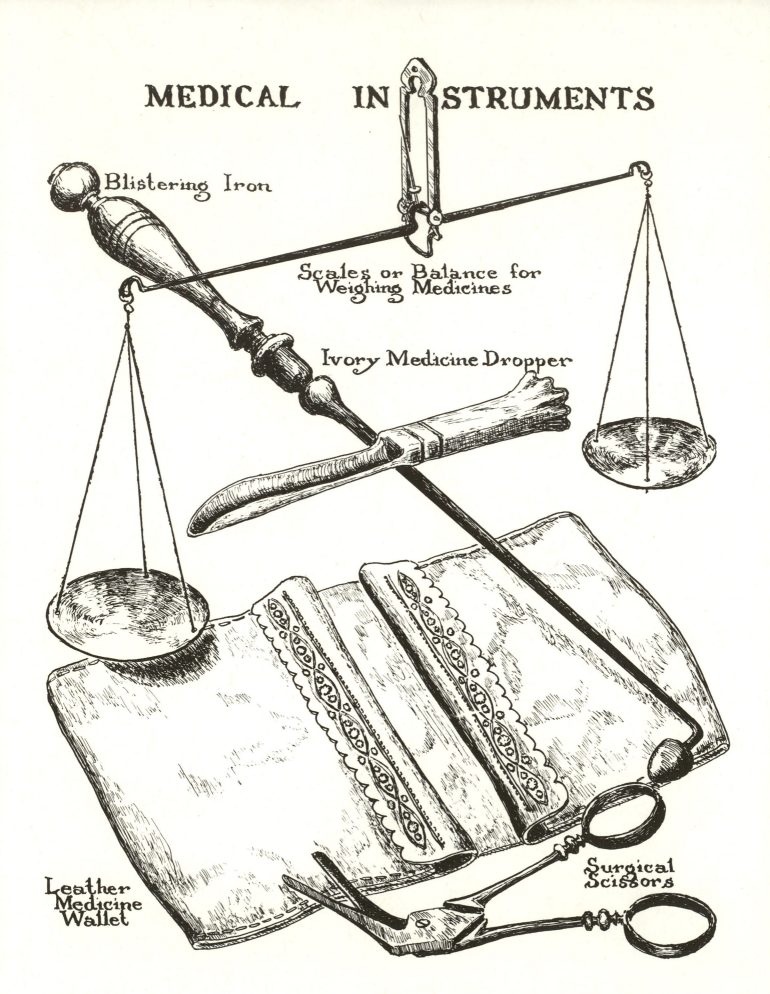

Blistering Iron

Scales or Balance for Weighing Medicines

Ivory Medicine Dropper

Leather Medicine Wallet

Surgical Scissors

SURGERY'S BIG THREE

Because anesthetics were unknown, the soldier made the best of his pain by chewing a lead bullet. This prevented the patient from crying out or biting his tongue.

Little was known of bodily functions, and the great cavities of the body were rarely opened by surgery. As a matter of fact, there were but three operative procedures practiced by the Continental Army physician.

1. TREPHINING ~ a cylindrical saw was used to remove a disc of bone, usually from the skull. Blood clots and pressure under the bone could be released through the hole made by this instrument.

2. AMPUTATION - the only major operation performed in the army. After severing an arm or leg, the stump was washed with hot tar. This most painful procedure cauterized the bleeding and sterilized the wound.

3. EXTRACTION OF MUSKET BALL - the ball was removed only if not beyond the reach of the finger. The cupped ends of the forceps grasped the lead sphere securely once it was located. If it lodged under the skin, an incision was made and the ball removed.

The wound was then brought together with plaster and bandage.

After surgery was completed, a dressing of soft flannel dipped in oil was applied, followed by a poultice of bread and milk. The inevitable bloodletting, gentle laxatives, warm baths and opium were also used.

CLEANLINESS IN CAMP

CLEANLINESS- Dr. Benjamin Rush observed, "Too much cannot be said in favor of cleanliness. If it were possible to convert every blade of grass on the continent into an American soldier, the want of cleanliness would reduce them in two or three campaigns to a handful of men." He recommended that the soldier wash his hands and face at least once daily, and the whole body two or three times weekly. Frequent changes of clean linen were equally important.

SHAVING - Regimental barbers obtained their own razors and soap, and with them shaved every soldier three times weekly. These services were paid for by the men, although sometimes grudgingly by those used to a less formal farm life.
  The camp day began when a sentry could see a thousand yards around him. This early hour gave little time for removing stubble, and the men were instructed to have their shaves in the evening, thereby being presentable for morning parade.

BATHING - During the warm hours of the day, between eight in the morning and five in the evening, bathing was discouraged. Remaining in the water was felt to be "too relaxing and injurious to health." Further, baths were not to be taken immediately following a march, but rather after the soldiers were rested and cool. Generally, bathing was best done in running water.

"SINKS" OR "NECESSARIES" - Quite logically, these were best located on the edge of a gully, or cliff. If the landscape lacked such accommodations, regimental sinks were dug no nearer than three hundred feet from the nearest occupied tent or hut. They were frequently covered by the previously removed soil. Every four days, and more often in warm weather, new sinks were shoveled.

HAIR

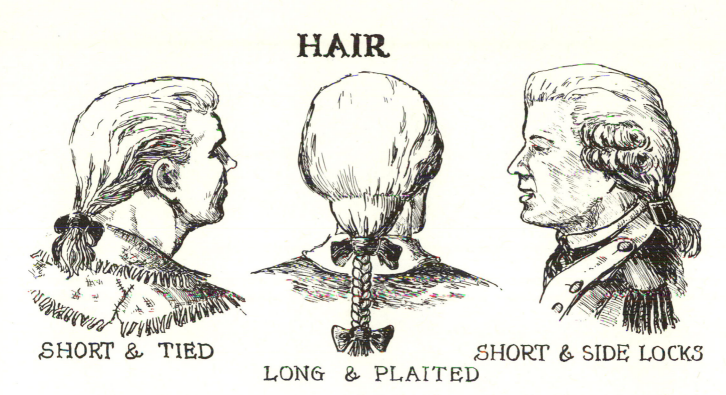

SHORT & TIED

LONG & PLAITED

SHORT & SIDE LOCKS

In contrast to ragged and patched uniforms, the soldiers' hair was kept trimmed and neat. In camp, the men in the ranks were required to powder their hair daily, and officers were to be freshly powdered for guard duty and ceremonies.

The Continentals favored two hair styles – short and tied or plaited (braided). The short cut was preferred, as was evident in a 1778 order to the First Carolina Line. The colonel wrote that he wished to have his men cut their hair short and called on his officers to set the example. "However some men may prize effeminate length of hair, short hair is certainly better for actual service."

Side locks with either style were much less popular than in civilian life. Only the most fastidious officer had the time or patience to bother with such niceties. After careful combing, the side hair must be rolled on curling paper over hot cylinders of pipe clay.

Regimental barbers were paid from the men's wages. In addition to furnishing hair cuts, they were asked to save fat and grease for hair dressing. This took considerable saving. A general inspection would require a half-pound of this "rendered tallow" as well as two pounds of flour for each hundred men.

Clay Hair Curler

Soldier's comb from sheet brass

Scissors

RELIGION IN CAMP

A rich spiritual life helped to balance the more material deficiencies of food, clothing, and weapons. Washington emphasized this when he said, "To the distinguished character of a Patriot, it should be our highest glory to add the more distinguished character of a Christian."

Prayers by the troops were an important part of the camp routine. They followed the reading of the daily orders and usually the roll call. On Sunday at eleven o'clock, the sermon was listened to with great interest and patriotic thoughts were often woven into the religious message. Prior to the service, the musicians marched forward and stacked their drums, one row on top of the other. These the minister used for his pulpit. Occasionally they were grouped to form a high platform on which the minister stood to deliver his message of hope and courage.

SHORTENING THE LONG CAMP DAY

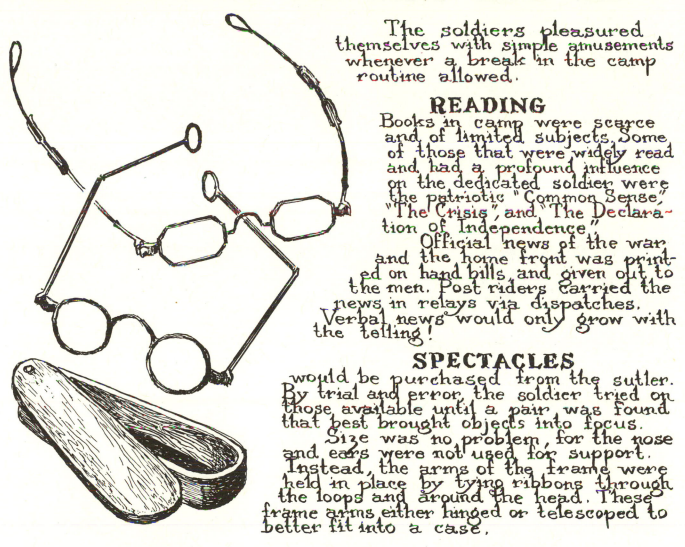

The soldiers pleasured themselves with simple amusements whenever a break in the camp routine allowed.

READING

Books in camp were scarce and of limited subjects. Some of those that were widely read and had a profound influence on the dedicated soldier were the patriotic "Common Sense," "The Crisis", and "The Declaration of Independence"

Official news of the war and the home front was printed on hand bills, and given out to the men. Post riders carried the news in relays via dispatches. Verbal news would only grow with the telling!

SPECTACLES

would be purchased from the sutler. By trial and error the soldier tried on those available until a pair was found that best brought objects into focus.

Size was no problem, for the nose and ears were not used for support. Instead, the arms of the frame were held in place by tying ribbons through the loops and around the head. These frame arms either hinged or telescoped to better fit into a case.

WRITING

As in civilian life, a completed letter was folded with the writing inside, then sealed together with a bit of hot wax. Occasionally a seal of some design was pressed into the cooling wax blob. Because there was no need for envelopes, the address was written on the outside of the letter.

A RELAXING PIPEFUL

The clay pipe was a popular item on the sutler's counter. To complete a relaxing combination, pipe tobacco could also be purchased. A popular style was "thread tobacco", made up of strands of the leaf and twisted into a rope-like hank. The soldier could buy whatever length his inflated Continental currency might permit.

The smoker sliced off a portion, ground it between palm and thumb, then packed his pipe for an aromatic smoke. It was all of that, for the leaves were liberally mixed with molasses, and sometimes licorice or vanilla.

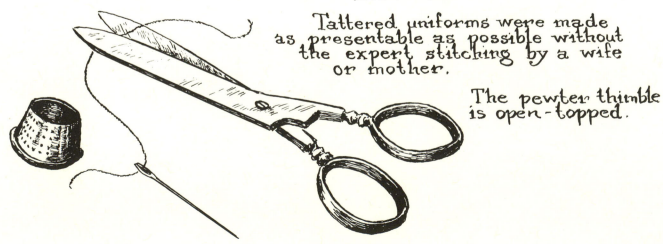

The above pipe was the most common design.

SEWING

Tattered uniforms were made as presentable as possible without the expert stitching by a wife or mother.

The pewter thimble is open-topped.

WHITTLING BONE AND WOOD

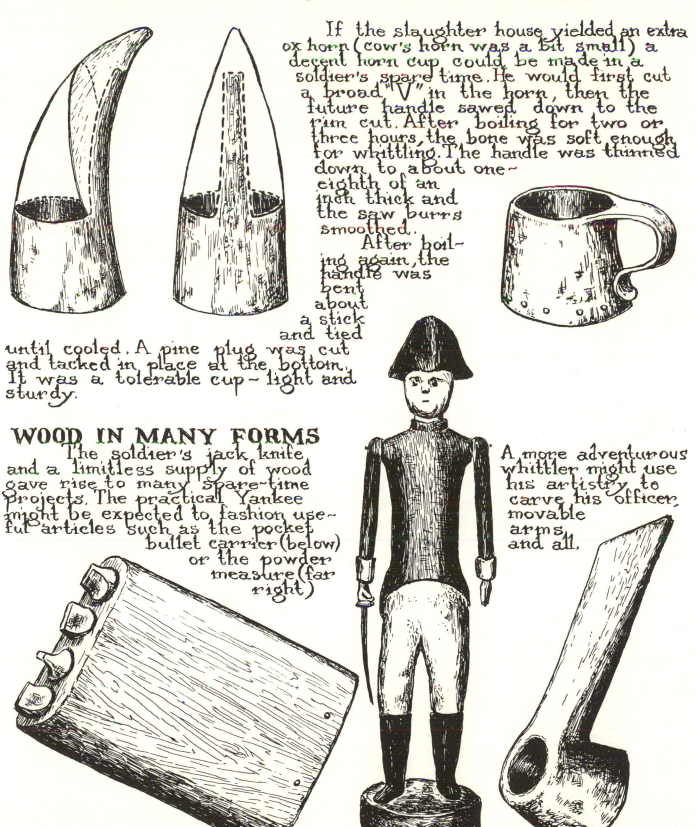

If the slaughter house yielded an extra ox horn (cow's horn was a bit small) a decent horn cup could be made in a soldier's spare time. He would first cut a broad "V" in the horn, then the future handle sawed down to the rim cut. After boiling for two or three hours, the bone was soft enough for whittling. The handle was thinned down to about one-eighth of an inch thick and the saw burrs smoothed.

After boiling again, the handle was bent about a stick and tied until cooled. A pine plug was cut and tacked in place at the bottom. It was a tolerable cup~ light and sturdy.

WOOD IN MANY FORMS

The soldier's jack knife and a limitless supply of wood gave rise to many spare-time projects. The practical Yankee might be expected to fashion use~ ful articles such as the pocket bullet carrier (below) or the powder measure (far right)

A more adventurous whittler might use his artistry to carve his officer, movable arms, and all.

85

CARVING CAMP WOODEN WARE

RIFLEMAN'S NOGGIN ~ Trees healed old scars by means of a gnarled growth, and from these burls, a rifleman could carve himself a handy noggin. The better burls were found on apple, cherry, maple, birch and oak trees. This section was sawed off close to the tree trunk, with a projection left on one side for the handle. With the wood "green" and more easily carved, the inside was whittled out – a curved chisel made this easier – after pilot holes were drilled.

Because the bark protected the outer surface, it was not removed until the inside of the cup was finished. To prevent checking and cracking, the modern-day whittler might soak the noggin overnight in linseed oil.. The handle was carved and drilled for a leather thong, and on the other end a wooden toggle was knotted in place. This was shoved under the rifleman's belt, and held there by pressure, ready for the first cool drink of spring water.

WOODEN DRINKING MUG ~ A circular series of holes was drilled into a block of hard wood. A mug-sized cylindrical hole was then carved out. The outside was roughly shaped with a chisel or tomahawk, then whittled smooth.

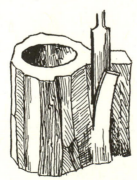

MORE ON SPARE TIME

The soldier in search of relaxation might spend an off hour fishing, hunting, or gathering a few tasty nuts for the evening meal. And if ice was on the river, skating was possible.

There were group diversions as well. Playing ball was popular, and the skill of tomahawk throwing or a "Rifle Frolic" was well worth watching. The winning marksman was treated to hard spirits by the losers.

The camp turned out for important visitors such as delegates to Congress or Indian chiefs to be hosted by the army. The soldiers viewed with great interest the British, Hessian and Tory prisoners as they passed through to confinement. Even funerals were a change of pace from the camp routine (and for the onlookers as well!)

Games included backgammon and darts. Gambling was strictly prohibited. Billiards and cards-and even the favorite "pitch penny"-were forbidden.

There were few forms of organized entertainment. One such was the theatrical performance in the Valley Forge bakehouse on April 15, 1778.

And if time still weighed heavily, one might pay attention to the soldier's best friend, the musket.

MULTIPURPOSE SCREWDRIVERS

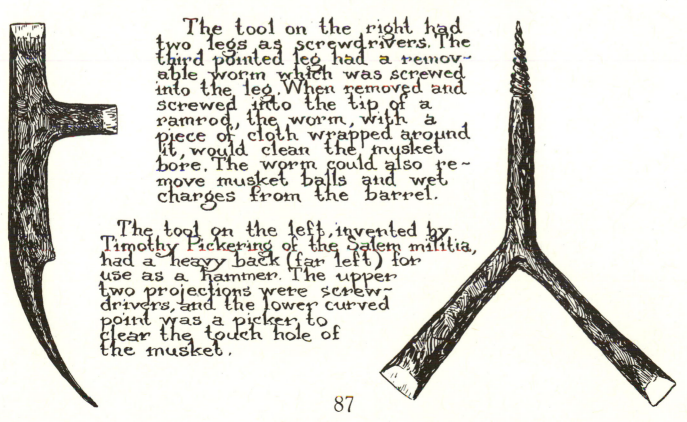

The tool on the right had two legs as screwdrivers. The third pointed leg had a removable worm which was screwed into the leg. When removed and screwed into the tip of a ramrod, the worm, with a piece of cloth wrapped around it, would clean the musket bore. The worm could also remove musket balls and wet charges from the barrel.

The tool on the left, invented by Timothy Pickering of the Salem militia, had a heavy back (far left) for use as a hammer. The upper two projections were screwdrivers, and the lower curved point was a picker to clear the touch hole of the musket.

CHILDREN'S PLAYTHINGS

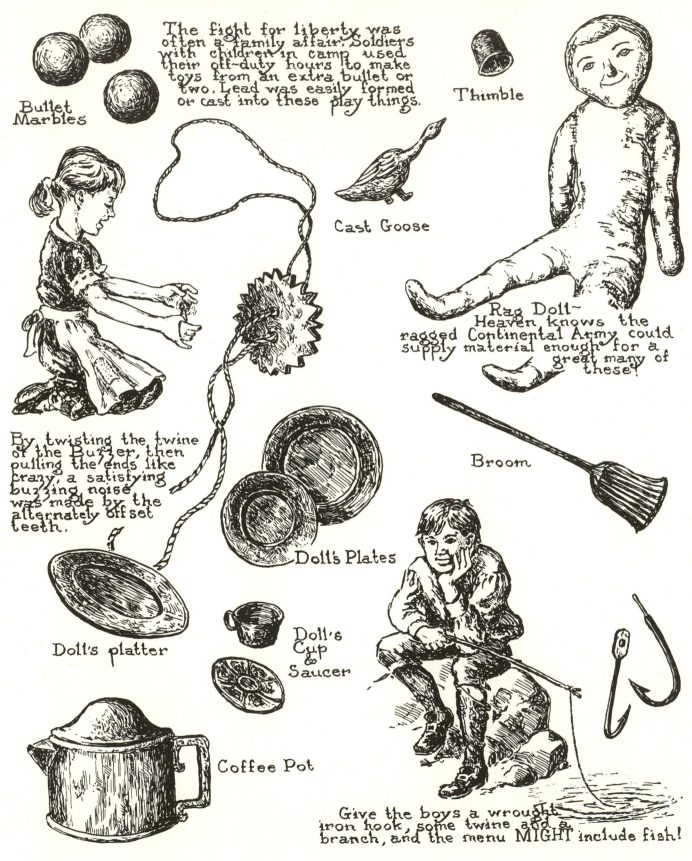

Bullet Marbles

The fight for liberty was often a family affair. Soldiers with children in camp used their off-duty hours to make toys from an extra bullet or two. Lead was easily formed or cast into these play things.

Thimble

Cast Goose

Rag Doll ~ Heaven knows the ragged Continental Army could supply material enough for a great many of these!

By twisting the twine of the Buzzer, then pulling the ends like crazy, a satisfying buzzing noise was made by the alternately offset teeth.

Doll's Plates

Broom

Doll's platter

Doll's Cup & Saucer

Coffee Pot

Give the boys a wrought iron hook, some twine and a branch, and the menu MIGHT include fish!

HOLIDAYS~THE GLORIOUS FOURTH

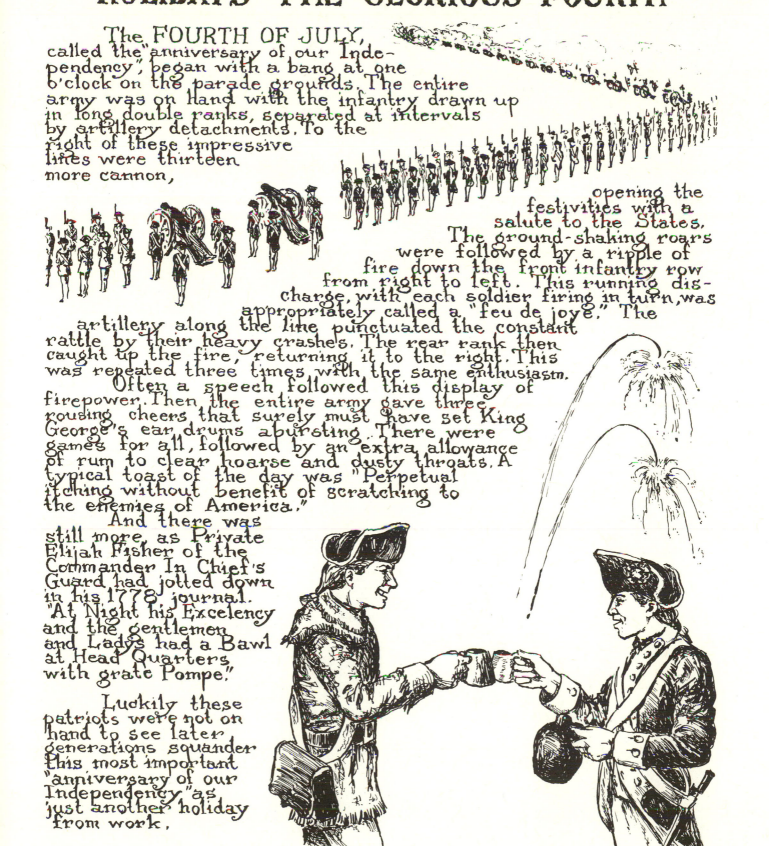

The FOURTH OF JULY, called the "anniversary of our Independency", began with a bang at one o'clock on the parade grounds. The entire army was on hand with the infantry drawn up in long double ranks, separated at intervals by artillery detachments. To the right of these impressive lines were thirteen more cannon, opening the festivities with a salute to the States. The ground-shaking roars were followed by a ripple of fire down the front infantry row from right to left. This running discharge, with each soldier firing in turn, was appropriately called a "feu de joye." The artillery along the line punctuated the constant rattle by their heavy crashes. The rear rank then caught up the fire, returning it to the right. This was repeated three times with the same enthusiasm.

Often a speech followed this display of firepower. Then the entire army gave three rousing cheers that surely must have set King George's ear drums abursting. There were games for all, followed by an extra allowance of rum to clear hoarse and dusty throats. A typical toast of the day was "Perpetual itching without benefit of scratching to the enemies of America."

And there was still more, as Private Elijah Fisher of the Commander In Chief's Guard had jotted down in his 1778 journal. "At Night his Excelency and the gentlemen and Lady's had a Bawl at Head Quarters with grate Pompe."

Luckily these patriots were not on hand to see later generations squander this most important "anniversary of our Independency" as just another holiday from work.

89

MORE HOLIDAYS

Days for the camp-weary soldier to remember:

NEW YEAR'S DAY, and a gill of spirits to start off the year.

ST. PATRICK'S DAY ~ Irish deserters from the King's army swelled the ranks of Irish-Americans until, at one point, they numbered one-third of the camp muster. The rugged brigade of Pennsylvania Continentals was often called "the line of Ireland."

At Valley Forge, New England troops needled their Irish friends with a disparaging stuffed figure of the Saint. Before Irish tempers could boil, Washington stepped in. "Well I, too, am a lover of St. Patrick's Day and must settle the affair by making all the army keep the day." Backing his convictions with action, he ordered an extra ration of rum for all. As an aide observed, "All made merry and were good friends."

MAY DAY - General Greene's Southern Army in 1782, lightheartedly welcomed the day with Maypoles and other festivities. As an observer noted, it was "something extraordinary" to think of battle-scarred veterans dancing gaily around a pole.

THANKSGIVING DAY - The troops fortified themselves against the long sermon with the extra ration of spirits.

CHRISTMAS - The sermon and extra spirits, together with greater liberties, made a welcome break in the camp routine. Christmas trees and bountiful fare were unknown, however, and if a soldier hung his stocking by the fireplace, it was only to dry out the winter dampness.

BATTLE CELEBRATIONS - For example, Congress gratefully sent thirty hogsheads of wine to the battle-weary fighters of Brandywine. Following Burgoyne's surrender, the pleasured troops fired cannon, shot sky rockets and generally made merry. France's entry into the war, as well as the arrival of French supplies, occasioned celebrations in camp.

Days for the soldier to forget:

KING'S BIRTHDAY - June 4th

KING'S CORONATION DAY - Or "King's Damnation Day" - September 22nd

AWARDS OF HONOR

The first national decoration for enlisted men was set in motion by Washington's orders on August 7th, 1782.

SERVICE STRIPES

Honored in these orders were soldiers "who have served more than three years with bravery, fidelity and good conduct; for this purpose a narrow piece of white cloth, of an angular form, is to be fixed to the left arm, on the uniform coat." Those serving the army faithfully for more than six years would wear two such angles of cloth.

THE PURPLE HEART
(THE BADGE OF MILITARY MERIT)

Washington's order continued with its most important announcements: "—when any singularly meritorious action is performed, the author of it shall be permitted to wear on his facings over his left breast, the figure of a heart in purple cloth, or silk edged with narrow lace or binding." Proof of such valorous deeds were to be certified by the commanding officers of the regiment and brigade and presented with the facts to the Commander in Chief.

If granted, the soldier's name, his regiment, and account of his deed were entered in the "Book of Merit". In addition to this, the wearer of the Purple Heart was presented a certificate and was permitted to pass all guards and sentinels by whom officers could pass.

SOCIETY OF THE CINCINNATI

In the spring of 1783, before the dispersion of the victorious Continental Army, the Society of the Cincinnati was formed. Conceived by General Knox and heartily approved by Washington, the Society embraced all officers of the Revolution. Its purpose was to perpetuate the deep friendships that had existed through those years of suffering and sacrifice, as well as uphold the democratic principles so recently won.

A handsome "Order" to distinguish these officers was a medal of gold "suspended by a deep blue ribbon two inches wide edges in white, descriptive of the union of America with France." The leaves of the olive branch were gold and green enamel, the head and tail of the eagle gold and white enamel and the sky in the center emblem of blue enamel. The latter showed the heroic Roman Cincinnatus receiving a sword and shield from three senators. Around the rim were the words, "Omnia relinquit servare rempublicam" or "He abandons every thing to serve his country."

Where to Find Examples of Relics Illustrated in this Book

(Note: Many of the articles in this list may be found in exhibits other than those mentioned, although those that are designated here contain particularly good examples. Most of the drawings in this book show items in the author's collection and have been verified by those seen elsewhere. Relics marked with an asterisk (*) are articles which, to the best of the author's knowledge, can only be found in those places indicated in this list but were well known to the Continental soldier.)

Relic and Page Location	Where to Find
*Silver eagle worn on Washington's hat cockade shown on p. 7	Mount Vernon, Mount Vernon, Va.
Hunting shirts on pp. 10 and 11	Washington's Headquarters State Historic Site, Newburgh, N.Y.; Fort Ticonderoga Museum, Ticonderoga, N.Y.
Overalls on pp. 10, 13, 14, 43, 53, and 55	Pattern given by Brigade of American Revolution to Sixth Massachusetts Continentals
Crested leather helmet, stock, coat, vest, overalls, French musket, waist cartridge box, bayonet, and canteen—all on p. 13	From previous display of life-size light infantry mannikin at the West Point Gallery, West Point, N.Y.
Uniform coat on p. 14	Pattern of the Sixth Massachusetts Continentals, compiled by George Snook, M.D., and William Wigham from (a) Detmar H. Finke and H. Charles McBarron, Jr., "Continental Army Uniform and Specifications 1779-1781," Military Collector & Historian, XIV, No. 2 (Summer 1962), 35-41, and (b) drawings supplied by Eric Manders; tailor's pattern of the Tench Tilghman coat, Maryland Historical Society, Baltimore, Md.
Breeches on p. 14	Bennington Museum, Bennington, Vt; Washington's Headquarters State Historic Site, Newburgh, N.Y.
French musket on p. 20	From previous display at the West Point Gallery, West Point, N.Y.
Muskets on p. 20	Smithsonian Institution, Washington, D.C.; Fort Ticonderoga Museum, Ticonderoga, N.Y.
Waist cartridge box on p. 24	Saratoga National Historical Park, Stillwater, N.Y.
*Tin cannister on p. 24	West Point Gallery, West Point, N.Y.
*Silver bullet on p. 26	Fort Ticonderoga Museum, Ticonderoga, N.Y.
Hunting shirt, leggings, belt, canteen, rifle, and powder horn—all on pp. 30 and 36	Saratoga National Historical Park, Stillwater, N.Y.
Pennsylvania or Kentucky rifle and powder horn on p. 31	Saratoga National Historical Park, Stillwater, N.Y.; previous display of life-size rifleman mannikin at the West Point Gallery, West Point, N.Y.
Hunting bag, knife, and sheath on p. 32	Saratoga National Historical Park, Stillwater, N.Y.; previous display of life-size rifleman mannikin at the West Point Gallery, West Point, N.Y.
Tomahawks on pp. 34 and 35	Saratoga National Historical Park, Stillwater, N.Y.; Valley Forge National Historical Park, Valley Forge, Pa.
Hat and knife in sheath on p. 37	Saratoga National Historical Park, Stillwater, N.Y.; previous display of life-size rifleman mannikin at the West Point Gallery, West Point, N.Y.
Lefthand fighting knife, ca. 1780, on p. 37	Loan by Capt. Foster Tallman on display at New Windsor Cantonment State Historic Site, Vails Gate, N.Y.
Lefthand rifle knife and center hunting knife on p. 37	Fort Ticonderoga Museum, Ticonderoga, N.Y.
Knife on p. 38	Saratoga National Historical Park, Stillwater, N.Y.; previous display of life-size rifleman mannikin at the West Point Gallery, West Point, N.Y.; Fort Ticonderoga Museum, Ticonderoga, N.Y.
Closed jack knife on p. 39	Saratoga National Historical Park, Stillwater, N.Y.
Leather saddle bags on p. 42	Peabody Institute, Salem, Mass.

Relic and Page Location	Where to Find
Lefthand wrought iron stirrup on p. 42	New York Historical Society Museum, Central Park W. at 77th St., New York, N.Y.
Silver spurs on p. 42	Mount Vernon, Mount Vernon, Va.
Iron fife on p. 48	Saratoga National Historical Park, Stillwater, N.Y.
Epaulettes on p. 50	Fort Ticonderoga Museum, Ticonderoga, N.Y.; Washington's Headquarters State Historic Site, Newburgh, N.Y.
Knapsack and haversack on p. 56	Fort Ticonderoga Museum, Ticonderoga, N.Y.; Memorial Hall Museum, Pocumtuck Valley Memorial Association, Deerfield, Mass.; Washington's Headquarters State Historic Site, Newburgh, N.Y.
Tin canteen on p. 56	Fort Ticonderoga Museum, Ticonderoga, N.Y.
Water bottles at top of p. 57	Bennington Museum, Bennington, Vt.; Memorial Museum, Pocumtuck Valley Memorial Museum Association, Deerfield, Mass.
*Monkey jug on p. 57	Memorial Hall Museum, Pocumtuck Valley Memorial Association, Deerfield, Mass.
Wooden canteen with handle at bottom of p. 57	Bennington Museum, Bennington, Vt.
*Brass and wrought iron candle holders on p. 59	Fort Ticonderoga Museum, Ticonderoga, N.Y.
*Old North Church lantern on p. 59	Concord Antiquarian House, Concord, Mass.
Iron kettles on pp. 8, 9, and 60	Peter Matteson Tavern, Shaftsbury, Vt.
Copper brazier on p. 61	Morristown National Historical Park, Morristown, N.J.
Camp stove on p. 61	Fort Ticonderoga Museum, Ticonderoga, N.Y.
Copper kettle on p. 61	Morristown National Historical Museum, Morristown, N.J.
Brass tent cooking pot on p. 61	Fort Ticonderoga Museum, Ticonderoga, N.Y.
Huts on pp. 66 and 67	Morristown National Historical Park, Morristown, N.J. Other soldiers' huts may be seen at Valley Forge National Historical Park, Valley Forge, Pa.
Common tent on p. 68	Diorama of Fort Independence at Fort Ticonderoga Museum, Ticonderoga, N.Y.
Markee on p. 68	Washington's headquarters tent, Smithsonian Institution, Washington, D.C.
Conestoga wagon on p. 72	Shelburne Museum, Shelburne, Vt.
Jefferson's spring lancet on p. 76	Monticello near Charlottesville, Va.
*Medical instruments on p. 78	Washington's Headquarters State Historic Site, Newburgh, N.Y.
Regimental barber's razor on p. 80	Washington's Headquarters State Historic Site, Newburgh, N.Y.
Scissors on p. 81	Fort Ticonderoga Museum, Ticonderoga, N.Y.
Pipes on p. 84	Essex Institute, Salem, Mass.; Saratoga National Historical Park, Stillwater, N.Y.
Thimble on p. 84	Fort Ticonderoga Museum, Ticonderoga, N.Y.
*Carved officer on p. 85	Shelburne Museum, Shelburne, Vt.
*Pocket bullet carrier on p. 85	Fort Ticonderoga Museum, Ticonderoga, N.Y.
*Wooden powder measure on p. 85	Essex Institute, Salem, Mass.
Righthand screwdrivers on p. 87	New York Historical Society Museum, Central Park W. at 77th St., New York, N.Y.
Purple Heart on p. 91	New Windsor Cantonment State Historic Site, Vails Gate, N.Y.

References

Adams, James Truslow, ed. in chief. *Album of American History*. New York: Charles Scribner's Sons, 1944.

Anburey, Thomas. *Travels*, London: 1789.

Beard, Daniel Carter. *Buckskin Book—For Buckskin Men and Boys*. Philadelphia and London: J. B. Lippincott Co., 1929.

————. *The Boy Pioneers—Sons of Daniel Boone*. New York: Charles Scribner's Sons, 1932.

Bird, Harrison K., Jr. "Early American Cavalry Helmets," *Bulletin of the Fort Ticonderoga Museum*, Vol. V, Serial No. 30 (July 1940).

Bolton, Charles Knowles. *The Private Soldier Under Washington*. Port Washington, N.Y.: Kennikat Press Inc., 1902.

Bowles and Carver. *Military Architecture Describing All Parts of a Fortification* (map in possession of Fort Ticonderoga Museum). London: mid-eighteenth century.

Bowman, Allen. *The Morale of the American Revolutionary Army*. Port Washington, N.Y.: Kennikat Press Inc., 1943.

Brockett, Frank S. "Note on Powder Horns," *Bulletin of the Fort Ticonderoga Museum*, IV, Serial No. 22 (May 1937), 93.

Calver, William Louis, and Bolton, Reginald Pelham. *History Written with Pick and Shovel*. New York: New York Historical Society, 1950.

Davis, Burke. *America's First Army*. A Colonial Williamsburg publication. New York: Holt, Rinehart & Winston, Inc., 1962.

Editors of *Life*. *America's Arts and Crafts*. New York: E. P. Dutton & Co., Inc.,1957.

Finke, Detmar H., and McBarron, H. Charles, Jr. "Continental Army Uniform and Specifications 1779–1781," *Military Collector & Historian*, XIV, No. 2 (Summer 1962), 35-41.

Fisher, Margaret. *Colonial America* (2nd ed.). Grand Rapids, Mich.: Fideler Co., 1962.

Fleming, Thomas J. "The Golden Door," *This Week* (the national Sunday magazine), February 20, 1966, pp. 2, 4–10, 12–14.

General Washington's Swords and Campaign Equipment (Catalogue Series No. 1). Mount Vernon, Va.: The Mount Vernon Ladies' Association, 1944 and 1947.

Goodman, Nathan G. *Benjamin Rush, Physician and Citizen*. Philadelphia: University of Pennsylvania Press, 1934.

Haywood, Arthur H. *Colonial Lighting*. New York: Dover Publications, Inc., 1962.

Held, Robert. *The Age of Firearms*. New York: Harper & Bros., 1957.

Historic Boston (pamphlet). Winchester, Mass.: Rawding Distributing Co., 1962.

Historical Preservations and Reconstructions. A reprint from *Park and Recreation Structures* (1938). Washington, D.C.: Department of the Interior, National Park Service, 1956.

Hume, Edgar Erskine. *Victories of Army Medicine*. Philadelphia, London, and Montreal: J.B. Lippincott Co., 1943.

Jaeger, Ellsworth. *Nature Crafts*. New York: Macmillan Co., 1961.

Ketchum, Richard M., ed. in charge. *The American Heritage Book of the Revolution*. New York: American Heritage Publishing Co., Inc., 1958.

Lattimer, John K. "An Exhibition of Silver Hilted Swords by American Silversmiths of the Colonial, Revolutionary and Federal Periods," *Bulletin of the Fort Ticonderoga Museum*, XI, No 6 (September 1965), 345-52.

————. "Sword Hilts by Early American Silversmiths," *Antiques*, February 1965, pp. 196-99.

Lefferts, Charles M. *Uniforms of the American, British, French, and German Armies in the War of the American Revolution, 1775–1783*. Edited by Alexander J. Wall, with an introduction by Dorothy C. Barck. A publication of the New York Historical Society. New York: J.J. Little & Ives Co., 1926.

Lossing, Benson J. *The Home of Washington*, New York: Virtue & Yorston, 1871.

McKearin, George S. and Helen. *American Glass*. New York: Crown Publishers, 1959.

Manucy, Albert. *Artillery Through the Ages*. (National Park Service Interpretive Series.) Washington: U.S. Printing Office, 1949 and 1962.

Martin, Joseph Plumb. *Private Yankee Doodle*. Edited by George F. Scheer. Boston and Toronto: Little, Brown & Co., 1962.

Marx, Rudolph. "A Medical Profile of George Washington," *The American Heritage Reader*. New York: Dell Publishing Co., Inc., 1956, pp. 21–38.

Mason, Bernard S. *Woodcraft*. New York: A.S. Barnes & Co., 1939.

Merkert, T.J. "The Toughest Thing on Wheels," *Boys' Life*, April 1966, p. 43.

Murray, Eleanor M. "The Medical Department of the Revolution," *Bulletin of the Fort Ticonderoga Museum*, VIII, No. 3 (January 1949), 83–109.

Nutting, Wallace. *Furniture Treasury*. New York: Macmillan Co., 1954.

Pell, Stephen H.P. "Notes on Pipes," *Bulletin of the Fort Ticonderoga Museum*, V, No. 4 (January 1940), 125.

————. "Poll Arms," *Bulletin of the Fort Ticonderoga Museum*, V, No. 3 (July 1939), 66–103.

————. "The Gorget," *Bulletin of the Fort Ticonderoga Museum*, IV, No. 5 (September 1937), 126–41.

————. "The Purple Heart," *Bulletin of the Fort Ticonderoga Museum*, VIII, No. 3 (January 1949), 113–14.

————. "The Silver Bullet," *Bulletin of the Fort Ticonderoga Museum*, IV, Serial No. 22 (May 1937), 94–97.

Peterson, Harold L. *American Indian Tomahawks*. A publication of the Museum of the American Indian, Heye Foundation. Gluckstadt, West Germany: J.J. Augustin, 1965.

————. *American Knives*. New York: Charles Scribner's Sons, 1958.

————. *Arms and Armor in Colonial America 1526–1783*. Harrisburg, Pa.: Stackpole Co., 1956.

————. *The Book of The Continental Soldier*. Harrisburg, Pa.: Stackpole Co., 1968.

————. *Forts in America*. New York: Charles Scribner's Sons, 1964.

Peterson, Mendel L. "American Epaulettes 1775–1820," *Military Collector & Historian*, II, No. 2 (June 1950), 17–21.

Pike, Thomas, "How to Make a Buckskin Outfit," *Muzzle Blasts*, February 1961, pp. 13–14.

Rush, Benjamin. Quotes from his "To the Officers in the Army of the United States: Directions for Preserving the Health of Soldiers," April 22, 1777, in "Benjamin Rush, Physician, and the Continental Army's Health—1777," *Scope Weekly*, IV, No. 26 (published for Upjohn Co., Kalamazoo, Mich., by Physicians News Service, Inc., July 1, 1959), 1–3.

Russell, Carl P. *Guns on the Early Frontiers*. Berkeley and Los Angeles: University of California Press, 1957.

St. George, Eleanor. *The Dolls of Yesterday*. New York: Charles Scribner's Sons, 1948.

Scheer, George F., and Rankin, Hugh F. *Rebels and Redcoats*. Cleveland and New York: World Publishing Co., 1957.

Sloane, Eric. *A Museum of Early American Tools*. New York: Wilfred Funk, Inc.,1964.

Steuben, Baron de. *Regulations for the Order and Discipline of the Troops of the United States*. Boston: Henry Ranlet for Thomas & Andrews, 1794.

Thacher, James. *Military Journal of the American Revolution*. Hartford, Conn.: Hurlburt, Williams & Co., 1862.

Tourtellot, Arthur Beron. *William Diamond's Drum*. New York: Doubleday & Co., 1959.

Tunis, Edwin. *Colonial Craftsmen*. Cleveland and New York: World Publishing Co., 1965.

————. *Colonial Living*. Cleveland and New York: World Publishing Co., 1965.

Webster, Donald B., Jr. *American Socket Bayonets 1717–1873*. A publication of the Museum Restoration Service, Ottawa, Ont.: Runge Press, 1964.

Weig, Melvin J. *Morristown: A Military Capital of the American Revolution*. ("Historical Handbook Series" of the National Park Service, No. 7.) Washington, D.C.: U.S. Government Printing Office, 1950 and 1957.

Wheeler, Robert F. "The American Belt Ax," *American Arms Collector*, I, No. 4 (October 1957), 127–30.

Wood, William, *The Winning of Freedom*. (*The Pageant of America*, ed. by Ralph Henry Gabriel, Vol. VI, Independence Edition.) New Haven: Yale University Press, 1927.

Woodward, Arthur. "The Metal Tomahawk," *Bulletin of the Fort Ticonderoga Museum*, VII, No. 3 (January 1946), 2–42.

Wright, John Womack. *Some Notes on the Continental Army* (Publication No. 2 of the New Windsor Cantonment for the National Temple Hill Association, Vails Gate, N.Y.). Cornwallville, N.Y.: Hope Farm Press, 1963.

Index